Ninja Foodi FlexDr

Fryer Cookbook 2024 UK

2000 Days of Flavorful and Crispy Air-Fried Ninja Dual Zone FlexDrawer Air Fryer AF500UK Recipes For Beginners & Advanced Using

Dorothy J. Fallon

CONTENTS

MEASUREMENT CONVERSIONS **13**

Breakfast Recipes **15**

Morning Patties 15

Buffalo Chicken Breakfast Muffins 15

Hash Browns 15

Quiche Breakfast Peppers 16

Wholemeal Banana-walnut Bread 16

Breakfast Sausage Omelet 16

Bacon Cheese Egg With Avocado And Potato Nuggets 17

Bacon Cinnamon Rolls 17

Quick And Easy Blueberry Muffins 18

Gyro Breakfast Patties With Tzatziki 18

Hard Boiled Eggs 18

Baked Egg And Mushroom Cups 19

Spinach Egg Muffins 19

Pepper Egg Cups 19

Morning Egg Rolls 20

Onion Omelette And Buffalo Egg Cups 20

Healthy Oatmeal Muffins 21

Crispy Hash Browns 21

Egg And Bacon Muffins 21

Cinnamon Apple French Toast 22

Mozzarella Bacon Calzones 22

Turkey Ham Muffins 22
Breakfast Meatballs 23
Baked Eggs 23
Sweet Potato Hash 23
Sausage & Butternut Squash 23
Air Fried Bacon And Eggs 24
Honey Banana Oatmeal 24
Red Pepper And Feta Frittata And Bacon Eggs On The Go 24
Brussels Sprouts Potato Hash 25
Eggs In Avocado Cups 25
Honey-apricot Granola With Greek Yoghurt 25
Asparagus And Bell Pepper Strata And Greek Bagels 26
Yellow Potatoes With Eggs 26
Spinach And Red Pepper Egg Cups With Coffee-glazed Canadian Bacon 27
Cinnamon Air Fryer Apples 27
Breakfast Sausage And Cauliflower 27
Air Fryer Sausage Patties 28
Bacon And Egg Omelet 28
Spinach And Swiss Frittata With Mushrooms 28
Snacks And Appetizers Recipes 29
Chicken Stuffed Mushrooms 29
Parmesan Crush Chicken 29
Kale Potato Nuggets 29
Crab Rangoon Dip With Crispy Wonton Strips 30
Shrimp Pirogues 30

Caramelized Onion Dip With White Cheese 31

Tater Tots 31

Avocado Fries 31

Five-ingredient Falafel With Garlic-yoghurt Sauce 32

Beefy Swiss Pastry 32

Parmesan Wings 33

Mozzarella Sticks 33

Bacon-wrapped Shrimp And Jalapeño 33

Parmesan French Fries 34

Mushroom Rolls 34

Fried Okra 34

Pepperoni Pizza Dip 35

Crispy Filo Artichoke Triangles 35

Cheese Corn Fritters 35

Healthy Spinach Balls 36

Vegetables And Sides Recipes 36

Air Fryer Vegetables 36

Bbq Corn 36

Stuffed Sweet Potatoes 37

Fried Asparagus 37

Curly Fries 37

Herb And Lemon Cauliflower 38

Air-fried Tofu Cutlets With Cacio E Pepe Brussels Sprouts 38

Falafel 39

Hasselback Potatoes 39

Kale And Spinach Chips 39
Air Fried Okra 40
Buffalo Bites 40
Fried Olives 40
Spanakopita Rolls With Mediterranean Vegetable Salad 41
Stuffed Tomatoes 41
Potato And Parsnip Latkes With Baked Apples 42
Rosemary Asparagus & Potatoes 42
Veggie Burgers With “fried” Onion Rings 43
Zucchini Cakes 43
Pepper Poppers 44
Sweet Potatoes With Honey Butter 44
Beef, Pork, And Lamb Recipes 45
Marinated Steak & Mushrooms 45
Garlic Butter Steak Bites 45
Breaded Pork Chops 45
Asian Pork Skewers 46
Steak In Air Fry 46
Steak And Mashed Creamy Potatoes 46
Tender Pork Chops 47
Pork With Green Beans And Potatoes 47
Garlic Sirloin Steak 47
Bbq Pork Loin 48
Italian Sausages With Peppers And Teriyaki Rump Steak With Broccoli 48
Beef Ribs Ii 49

Honey Glazed Bbq Pork Ribs 49
Simple Beef Sirloin Roast 49
Curry-crusted Lamb Chops With Baked Brown Sugar Acorn Squash 50
Cheesy Low-carb Lasagna 50
Simple Lamb Meatballs 51
Roasted Beef 51
Hot Dogs Wrapped In Bacon 51
Meatballs 51
Cinnamon-beef Kofta 52
Goat Cheese-stuffed Bavette Steak 52
Beef & Broccoli 52
Cinnamon-apple Pork Chops 53
Taco Seasoned Steak 53
Meat And Rice Stuffed Peppers 53
Green Pepper Cheeseburgers 54
Mongolian Beef With Sweet Chili Brussels Sprouts 54
Italian-style Meatballs With Garlicky Roasted Broccoli 55
Pork Tenderloin With Brown Sugar–pecan Sweet Potatoes 55
Chipotle Beef 56
Easy Breaded Pork Chops 56
Scallops With Greens 56
Mustard Pork Chops 57
Mustard Rubbed Lamb Chops 57

Fish And Seafood Recipes 57

Cod With Jalapeño 57

Fried Prawns 58
Tilapia With Mojo And Crispy Plantains 58
Tuna Patties With Spicy Sriracha Sauce Coconut Prawns 59
Lemon Pepper Fish Fillets 59
Basil Cheese Salmon 59
South Indian Fried Fish 60
Flavorful Salmon With Green Beans 60
Spicy Salmon Fillets 60
Lemon Pepper Salmon With Asparagus 61
Cajun Scallops 61
Herbed Prawns Pita 61
Honey Teriyaki Salmon 62
Scallops And Spinach With Cream Sauce And Confetti Salmon Burgers 62
Broiled Teriyaki Salmon With Eggplant In Stir-fry Sauce 63
Snapper Scampi 63
Blackened Red Snapper 63
Crumb-topped Sole 64
Dukkah-crusted Halibut 64
Fish And Chips 64
Crusted Cod 65
Beer Battered Fish Fillet 65
Chili Honey Salmon 65
Salmon Nuggets 66
Simple Buttery Cod & Salmon On Bed Of Fennel And Carrot 66
Perfect Parmesan Salmon 66

Butter-wine Baked Salmon 67

Crusted Shrimp 67

Chili Lime Tilapia 67

Stuffed Mushrooms With Crab 68

Two-way Salmon 68

Crispy Fish Nuggets 68

Sesame Honey Salmon 69

Southwestern Fish Fillets 69

Parmesan-crusted Fish Sticks With Baked Macaroni And Cheese 69

Cod With Avocado And Garlic Prawns 70

Prawn Dejonghe Skewers 71

Crispy Parmesan Cod 71

Frozen Breaded Fish Fillet 71

Poultry Recipes 72

Spice-rubbed Chicken Pieces 72

Chicken Fajitas With Street Corn 72

Chicken Potatoes 73

Simply Terrific Turkey Meatballs 73

Honey Butter Chicken 73

Chicken And Vegetable Fajitas 74

Whole Chicken 74

Juicy Paprika Chicken Breast 74

Bang-bang Chicken 75

Chicken With Pineapple And Peach 75

Curried Orange Honey Chicken 75

General Tso's Chicken 76
Air Fried Chicken Potatoes With Sun-dried Tomato 76
Chicken Wings With Piri Piri Sauce 77
Spicy Chicken Sandwiches With "fried" Pickles 77
Chicken Strips With Satay Sauce 78
Broccoli Cheese Chicken 78
Chicken Breast Strips 79
Delicious Chicken Skewers 79
Greek Chicken Souvlaki 79
Jerk Chicken Thighs 80
Turkey Burger Patties 80
Thai Curry Chicken Kabobs 80
Bacon-wrapped Chicken 81
Pickled Chicken Fillets 81
Turkey And Cranberry Quesadillas 82
Dijon Chicken Wings 82
Thai Chicken Meatballs 82
Chicken And Broccoli 83
Chili Chicken Wings 83
Chicken Parmesan With Roasted Lemon-parmesan Broccoli 84
Crusted Chicken Breast 84
Pretzel Chicken Cordon Bleu 85
Stuffed Chicken Florentine 85
Broccoli And Cheese Stuffed Chicken 85
Yummy Chicken Breasts 86

Garlic Dill Wings 86

Spiced Chicken And Vegetables 86

Chicken Tenders And Curly Fries 87

Wings With Corn On Cob 87

Herbed Turkey Breast With Simple Dijon Sauce 87

Chicken Legs With Leeks 88

Desserts Recipes 88

Double Chocolate Brownies 88

Pumpkin Muffins With Cinnamon 88

Zesty Cranberry Scones 89

Victoria Sponge Cake 89

Moist Chocolate Espresso Muffins 90

Cinnamon Sugar Dessert Fries 90

Sweet Protein Powder Doughnut Holes 90

Coconut Muffins And Dark Chocolate Lava Cake 91

Air Fried Bananas 91

Citrus Mousse 91

Molten Chocolate Almond Cakes 92

Stuffed Apples 92

Chocolate Pudding 92

Spiced Apple Cake 93

Chocolate Cookies 93

Butter Cake 93

S'mores Dip With Cinnamon-sugar Tortillas 94

Easy Mini Chocolate Chip Pan Cookie 94

MEASUREMENT CONVERSIONS

BASIC KITCHEN CONVERSIONS & EQUIVALENTS

DRY MEASUREMENTS CONVERSION CHART

3 TEASPOONS = 1 TABLESPOON = 1/16 CUP
6 TEASPOONS = 2 TABLESPOONS = 1/8 CUP
12 TEASPOONS = 4 TABLESPOONS = 1/4 CUP
24 TEASPOONS = 8 TABLESPOONS = 1/2 CUP
36 TEASPOONS = 12 TABLESPOONS = 3/4 CUP
48 TEASPOONS = 16 TABLESPOONS = 1 CUP

METRIC TO US COOKING CONVER-SIONS

OVEN TEMPERATURES

120 °C = 250 °F
160 °C = 320 °F
180 °C = 350 °F
205 °C = 400 °F
220 °C = 425 °F

LIQUID MEASUREMENTS CONVERSION CHART

8 FLUID OUNCES = 1 CUP = 1/2 PINT = 1/4 QUART
16 FLUID OUNCES = 2 CUPS = 1 PINT = 1/2 QUART
32 FLUID OUNCES = 4 CUPS = 2 PINTS = 1 QUART
1/4 GALLON
128 FLUID OUNCES = 16 CUPS = 8 PINTS = 4 QUARTS = 1 GALLON

BAKING IN GRAMS

1 CUP FLOUR = 140 GRAMS
1 CUP SUGAR = 150 GRAMS
1 CUP POWDERED SUGAR=160 GRAMS
1 CUP HEAVY CREAM = 235 GRAMS

VOLUME

1 MILLILITER=1/5 TEASPOON
5 ML = 1 TEASPOON
15 ML = 1 TABLESPOON
240 ML = 1 CUP OR 8 FLUID OUNCES
1 LITER=34 FL. OUNCES

WEIGHT

1 GRAM = 035 OUNCES
100 GRAMS=3.5 OUNCES
500 GRAMS = 1.1 POUNDS
1 KILOGRAM=35 OUNCES

US TO METRIC COOKING CONVERSIONS

1/5 TSP = 1 ML
1 TSP=5 ML
1 TBSP = 15 ML
1 FL OUNCE = 30 ML
1 CUP=237 ML
1 PINT (2 CUPS) = 473 ML
1 QUART (4 CUPS)=.95 LITER
1GALLON (16 CUPS)=3.8LITERS
1 0Z=28 GRAMS
1 POUND = 454 GRAMS

BUTTER

1 CUP BUTTER=2 STICKS = 8 OUNCES = 230 GRAMS=8 TABLESPOONS

WHAT DOES 1 CUP EQUAL

1 CUP = 8 FLUID OUNCES
1 CUP = 16 TABLESPOONS
1 CUP = 48 TEASPOONS
1 CUP = 1/2 PINT
1 CUP = 1/4 QUART
1 CUP = 1/16 GALLON
1 CUP = 240 ML

BAKING PAN CONVERSIONS

1 CUP ALL-PURPOSE FLOUR=4.5 OZ
1 CUP ROLLED OATS = 3 OZ 1 LARGE EGG = 1.7 OZ
1 CUP BUTTER=80Z 1 CUP MILK = 8 OZ
1 CUP HEAVY CREAM = 8.4 OZ
1 CUP GRANULATED SUGAR=7.1 OZ
1 CUP PACKED BROWN SUGAR = 7.75 OZ
1 CUP VEGETABLE OIL = 7.7 OZ
1 CUP UNSIFTED POWDERED SUGAR = 4.4 OZ

BAKING PAN CONVERSIONS

9-INCH ROUND CAKE PAN= 12 CUPS
10-INCH TUBE PAN =16 CUPS
11-INCH BUNDT PAN = 12 CUPS
9-INCH SPRINGFORM PAN = 10 CUPS
9 X 5 INCH LOAF PAN=8 CUPS
9-INCH SQUARE PAN=8 CUPS

Breakfast Recipes

Morning Patties

Servings: 4
Cooking Time: 13 Minutes.

Ingredients:

- 1 lb. minced pork
- 1 lb. minced turkey
- 2 teaspoons dry rubbed sage
- 2 teaspoons fennel seeds
- 2 teaspoons garlic powder
- 1 teaspoon paprika
- 1 teaspoon of sea salt
- 1 teaspoon dried thyme

Directions:

1. In a mixing bowl, add turkey and pork, then mix them together.
2. Mix sage, fennel, paprika, salt, thyme, and garlic powder in a small bowl.
3. Drizzle this mixture over the meat mixture and mix well.
4. Take 2 tablespoons of this mixture at a time and roll it into thick patties.
5. Place half of the patties in Zone 1, and the other half in Zone 2, then spray them all with cooking oil.
6. Return the crisper plate to the Ninja Foodi Dual Zone Air Fryer.
7. Choose the Air Fry mode for Zone 1 and set the temperature to 390 degrees F and the time to 13 minutes.
8. Select the "MATCH" button to copy the settings for Zone 2.
9. Initiate cooking by pressing the START/STOP button.
10. Flip the patties in the drawers once cooked halfway through.
11. Serve warm and fresh.

Nutrition:

- (Per serving) Calories 305 | Fat 25g |Sodium 532mg | Carbs 2.3g | Fiber 0.4g | Sugar 2g | Protein 18.3g

Buffalo Chicken Breakfast Muffins

Servings: 10
Cooking Time: 13 To 16 Minutes

Ingredients:

- 170 g shredded cooked chicken
- 85 g blue cheese, crumbled
- 2 tablespoons unsalted butter, melted
- 80 ml Buffalo hot sauce, such as Frank's RedHot
- 1 teaspoon minced garlic
- 6 large eggs
- Sea salt and freshly ground black pepper, to taste
- Avocado oil spray

Directions:

1. In a large bowl, stir together the chicken, blue cheese, melted butter, hot sauce, and garlic.
2. In a medium bowl or large liquid measuring cup, beat the eggs. Season with salt and pepper.
3. Spray 10 silicone muffin cups with oil. Divide the chicken mixture among the cups, and pour the egg mixture over top.
4. Place the cups in the two air fryer baskets and set to 150°C. Bake for 13 to 16 minutes, until the muffins are set and cooked through.

Hash Browns

Servings: 4
Cooking Time: 5 Minutes

Ingredients:

- 4 frozen hash browns patties
- Cooking oil spray of choice

Directions:

1. Install a crisper plate in both drawers. Place half the hash browns in zone 1 and half in zone 2, then insert the drawers into the unit. Spray the hash browns with some cooking oil.
2. Select zone 1, select AIR FRY, set temperature to 390 degrees F/ 200 degrees C, and set time to 5 minutes.
3. Select MATCH to match zone 2 settings to zone 1. Press the START/STOP button to begin cooking.
4. When cooking is complete, remove the hash browns and serve.

Nutrition:

- (Per serving) Calories 130 | Fat 7g | Sodium 300mg | Carbs 15g | Fiber 2g | Sugar 0g | Protein 1g

Quiche Breakfast Peppers

Servings: 4
Cooking Time: 15 Minutes
Ingredients:

- 4 eggs
- ½ tsp garlic powder
- 112g mozzarella cheese, shredded
- 125g ricotta cheese
- 2 bell peppers, cut in half & remove seeds
- 7½g baby spinach, chopped
- 22g parmesan cheese, grated
- ¼ tsp dried parsley

Directions:

1. In a bowl, whisk eggs, ricotta cheese, garlic powder, parsley, cheese, and spinach.
2. Pour the egg mixture into each bell pepper half and top with mozzarella cheese.
3. Insert a crisper plate in the Ninja Foodi air fryer baskets.
4. Place bell peppers in both the baskets.
5. Select zone 1 then select "air fry" mode and set the temperature to 355 degrees F for 15 minutes. Press "match" to match zone 2 settings to zone 1. Press "start/stop" to begin.

Nutrition:

- (Per serving) Calories 136 | Fat 7.6g |Sodium 125mg | Carbs 6.9g | Fiber 0.9g | Sugar 3.5g | Protein 10.8g

Wholemeal Banana-walnut Bread

Servings: 6
Cooking Time: 23 Minutes
Ingredients:

- Olive oil cooking spray
- 2 ripe medium bananas
- 1 large egg
- 60 ml non-fat plain Greek yoghurt
- 60 ml olive oil
- ½ teaspoon vanilla extract
- 2 tablespoons honey
- 235 ml wholemeal flour
- ¼ teaspoon salt
- ¼ teaspoon baking soda
- ½ teaspoon ground cinnamon
- 60 ml chopped walnuts

Directions:

1. Lightly coat the inside of two 5 ½-by-3-inch loaf pans with olive oil cooking spray.
2. In a large bowl, mash the bananas with a fork. Add the egg, yoghurt, olive oil, vanilla, and honey. Mix until well combined and mostly smooth. Sift the wholemeal flour, salt, baking soda, and cinnamon into the wet mixture, then stir until just combined. Do not overmix. Gently fold in the walnuts. Pour into the prepared loaf pans and spread to distribute evenly.
3. Place a loaf pan in the zone 1 drawer and another pan into zone 2 drawer. In zone 1, select Bake button and adjust temperature to 180°C, set time to 20 to 23 minutes. In zone 2, select Match Cook and press Start.
4. Remove until golden brown on top and a toothpick inserted into the center comes out clean. Allow to cool for 5 minutes before serving.

Breakfast Sausage Omelet

Servings:2
Cooking Time:8
Ingredients:

- ¼ pound breakfast sausage, cooked and crumbled
- 4 eggs, beaten
- ½ cup pepper Jack cheese blend
- 2 tablespoons green bell pepper, sliced
- 1 green onion, chopped
- 1 pinch cayenne pepper
- Cooking spray

Directions:

1. Take a bowl and whisk eggs in it along with crumbled sausage, pepper Jack cheese, green onions, red bell pepper, and cayenne pepper.
2. Mix it all well.
3. Take two cake pans that fit inside the air fryer and grease it with oil spray.
4. Divide the omelet mixture between cake pans.
5. Put the cake pans inside both of the Ninja Foodie 2-Basket Air Fryer baskets.
6. Turn on the BAKE function of the zone 1 basket and let it cook for 15-20 minutes at 310 degrees F.
7. Select MATCH button for zone 2 basket.
8. Once the cooking cycle completes, take out, and serve hot, as a delicious breakfast.

Nutrition:

- (Per serving) Calories 691| Fat52.4g | Sodium1122 mg | Carbs 13.3g | Fiber 1.8g| Sugar 7g | Protein 42g

Bacon Cheese Egg With Avocado And Potato Nuggets

Servings: 8

Cooking Time: 20 Minutes

Ingredients:

- Bacon Cheese Egg with Avocado:
- 6 large eggs
- 60 ml double cream
- 350 ml chopped cauliflower
- 235 ml shredded medium Cheddar cheese
- 1 medium avocado, peeled and pitted
- 8 tablespoons full-fat sour cream
- 2 spring onions, sliced on the bias
- 12 slices bacon, cooked and crumbled
- Potato Nuggets:
- 1 teaspoon extra virgin olive oil
- 1 clove garlic, minced
- 1 L kale, rinsed and chopped
- 475 ml potatoes, boiled and mashed
- 30 ml milk
- Salt and ground black pepper, to taste
- Cooking spray

Directions:

1. Make the Bacon Cheese Egg with Avocado :
2. In a medium bowl, whisk eggs and cream together. Pour into a round baking dish.
3. Add cauliflower and mix, then top with Cheddar. Place dish into the zone 1 air fryer drawer.
4. Adjust the temperature to 160°C and set the timer for 20 minutes.
5. When completely cooked, eggs will be firm and cheese will be browned. Slice into four pieces.
6. Slice avocado and divide evenly among pieces. Top each piece with 2 tablespoons sour cream, sliced spring onions, and crumbled bacon.
7. Make the Potato Nuggets :
8. Preheat the zone 2 air fryer drawer to 200°C.
9. In a skillet over medium heat, sauté the garlic in the olive oil, until it turns golden brown. Sauté with the kale for an additional 3 minutes and remove from the heat.
10. Mix the mashed potatoes, kale and garlic in a bowl. Pour in the milk and sprinkle with salt and pepper.
11. Shape the mixture into nuggets and spritz with cooking spray.
12. Put in the zone 2 air fryer drawer and air fry for 15 minutes, flip the nuggets halfway through cooking to make sure the nuggets fry evenly.
13. Serve immediately.

Bacon Cinnamon Rolls

Servings: 8

Cooking Time: 10 Minutes

Ingredients:

- 8 bacon strips
- 180ml bourbon
- 1 tube (310g) refrigerated cinnamon rolls with icing
- 55g chopped pecans
- 2 tablespoons maple syrup

Directions:

1. In a small bowl, combine the bacon and the bourbon. Refrigerate overnight after sealing. Remove the bacon and pat it dry; toss out the bourbon.
2. Cook bacon in batches in a large frying pan over medium heat until nearly crisp but still flexible. Remove to a plate lined with paper towels to drain.
3. Separate the dough into 8 rolls and set aside the frosting packet. Spiral rolls should be unrolled into long strips.
4. Place 1 bacon strip on each dough strip, cut as necessary, and reroll to form a spiral. To seal the ends, pinch them together.
5. Press your chosen zone - "Zone 1" or "Zone 2" and then rotate the knob to select "Air Fry".
6. Set the temperature to 175 degrees C, and then set the time for 5 minutes to preheat.
7. After preheating, spray the Air-Fryer basket of each zone with cooking spray, line them with parchment paper, and place rolls.
8. Slide the basket into the Air Fryer and set the time for 5 minutes.
9. Turn the rolls over and cook for another 4 minutes, or until golden brown.
10. Meanwhile, combine the pecans and maple syrup in a mixing bowl. In a separate bowl, combine the contents of the icing packet.
11. Heat the remaining bacon drippings in the same frying pan over medium heat. Cook, stirring regularly until the pecan mixture is gently browned, about 2-3 minutes.
12. After cooking time is completed, transfer them onto serving plates and drizzle half the icing over warm cinnamon rolls; top with half the pecans.

Quick And Easy Blueberry Muffins

Servings: 8 Muffins
Cooking Time: 12 Minutes
Ingredients:

- 315 ml flour
- 120 ml sugar
- 2 teaspoons baking powder
- ¼ teaspoon salt
- 80 ml rapeseed oil
- 1 egg
- 120 ml milk
- 160 ml blueberries, fresh or frozen and thawed

Directions:

1. Preheat the air fryer to 165°C.
2. In a medium bowl, stir together flour, sugar, baking powder, and salt.
3. In a separate bowl, combine oil, egg, and milk and mix well.
4. Add egg mixture to dry ingredients and stir just until moistened.
5. Gently stir in the blueberries.
6. Spoon batter evenly into parchment paper-lined muffin cups.
7. Put the muffin cups in the two air fryer baskets and bake for 12 minutes or until tops spring back when touched lightly.
8. Serve immediately.

Gyro Breakfast Patties With Tzatziki

Servings: 16
Cooking Time: 20 Minutes
Ingredients:

- patties
- Patties:
- 900 g lamb or beef mince
- 120 ml diced red onions
- 60 ml sliced black olives
- 2 tablespoons tomato sauce
- 1 teaspoon dried oregano leaves
- 2 cloves garlic, minced
- 1 teaspoon fine sea salt
- Tzatziki:
- 235 ml full-fat sour cream
- 1 small cucumber, chopped
- ½ teaspoon fine sea salt
- ½ teaspoon garlic powder, or 1 clove garlic, minced
- ¼ teaspoon dried dill, or 1 teaspoon finely chopped fresh dill
- For Garnish/Serving:
- 120 ml crumbled feta cheese (about 60 g)
- Diced red onions
- Sliced black olives
- Sliced cucumbers

Directions:

1. Preheat the air fryer to 176°C. 2. Place the lamb, onions, olives, tomato sauce, oregano, garlic, and salt in a large bowl. Mix well to combine the ingredients. 3. Using your hands, form the mixture into sixteen 3-inch patties. Place the patties in the two air fryer drawers and air fry for 20 minutes, flipping halfway through. Remove the patties and place them on a serving platter. 4. While the patties cook, make the tzatziki: Place all the ingredients in a small bowl and stir well. Cover and store in the fridge until ready to serve. Garnish with ground black pepper before serving. 5. Serve the patties with a dollop of tzatziki, a sprinkle of crumbled feta cheese, diced red onions, sliced black olives, and sliced cucumbers. 6. Store leftovers in an airtight container in the refrigerator for up to 5 days or in the freezer for up to a month. Reheat the patties in a preheated 200°C air fryer for a few minutes, until warmed through.

Hard Boiled Eggs

Servings: 6
Cooking Time: 18 Minutes
Ingredients:

- 6 eggs
- Cold water

Directions:

1. Press your chosen zone - "Zone 1" or "Zone 2" and then rotate the knob to select "Air Fryer".
2. Set the temperature to 120 degrees C, and then set the time for 5 minutes to preheat.
3. After preheating, arrange eggs into the basket of each zone.
4. Slide the baskets into Air Fryer and set the time for 18 minutes.
5. After cooking time is completed, transfer the eggs into cold water and serve.

Baked Egg And Mushroom Cups

Servings: 6
Cooking Time: 15 Minutes
Ingredients:

- Olive oil cooking spray
- 6 large eggs
- 1 garlic clove, minced
- ½ teaspoon salt
- ½ teaspoon black pepper
- Pinch red pepper flakes
- 230 g baby mushrooms, sliced
- 235 ml fresh baby spinach
- 2 spring onions, white parts and green parts, diced

Directions:

1. Lightly coat the inside of six silicone muffin cups or a six-cup muffin tin with olive oil cooking spray. In a large bowl, beat the eggs, garlic, salt, pepper, and red pepper flakes for 1 to 2 minutes, or until well combined.
2. Fold in the mushrooms, spinach, and spring onions. Divide the mixture evenly among the muffin cups. Place into the zone 1 drawer.
3. Select Bake button and adjust temperature to 160°C, set time to 12 to 15 minutes and press Start. Remove after the end and allow to cool for 5 minutes before serving.

Spinach Egg Muffins

Servings: 4
Cooking Time: 13 Minutes.
Ingredients:

- 4 tablespoons milk
- 4 tablespoons frozen spinach, thawed
- 4 large eggs
- 8 teaspoons grated cheese
- Salt, to taste
- Black pepper, to taste
- Cooking Spray

Directions:

1. Grease four small-sized ramekin with cooking spray.
2. Add egg, cheese, spinach, and milk to a bowl and beat well.
3. Divide the mixture into the four small ramekins and top them with salt and black pepper.
4. Place the two ramekins in each of the two crisper plate.
5. Return the crisper plate to the Ninja Foodi Dual Zone Air Fryer.
6. Choose the Air Fry mode for Zone 1 and set the temperature to 390 degrees F and the time to 13 minutes.
7. Select the "MATCH" button to copy the settings for Zone 2.
8. Initiate cooking by pressing the START/STOP button.
9. Serve warm.

Nutrition:

- (Per serving) Calories 237 | Fat 19g |Sodium 518mg | Carbs 7g | Fiber 1.5g | Sugar 3.4g | Protein 12g

Pepper Egg Cups

Servings: 4
Cooking Time: 18 Minutes.
Ingredients:

- 2 halved bell pepper, seeds removed
- 4 eggs
- 1 teaspoon olive oil
- 1 pinch salt and black pepper
- 1 pinch sriracha flakes

Directions:

1. Slice the bell peppers in half, lengthwise, and remove their seeds and the inner portion to get a cup-like shape.
2. Rub olive oil on the edges of the bell peppers.
3. Place them in the two crisper plates with their cut side up and crack 1 egg in each half of bell pepper.
4. Drizzle salt, black pepper, and sriracha flakes on top of the eggs.
5. Return the crisper plates to the Ninja Foodi Dual Zone Air Fryer.
6. Choose the Air Fry mode for Zone 1 and set the temperature to 390 degrees F and the time to 18 minutes.
7. Select the "MATCH" button to copy the settings for Zone 2.
8. Initiate cooking by pressing the START/STOP button.
9. Serve warm and fresh.

Nutrition:

- (Per serving) Calories 183 | Fat 15g |Sodium 402mg | Carbs 2.5g | Fiber 0.4g | Sugar 1.1g | Protein 10g

Morning Egg Rolls

Servings: 6
Cooking Time: 13 Minutes.

Ingredients:

- 2 eggs
- 2 tablespoons milk
- Salt, to taste
- Black pepper, to taste
- ½ cup shredded cheddar cheese
- 2 sausage patties
- 6 egg roll wrappers
- 1 tablespoon olive oil
- 1 cup water

Directions:

1. Grease a small skillet with some olive oil and place it over medium heat.
2. Add sausage patties and cook them until brown.
3. Chop the cooked patties into small pieces. Beat eggs with salt, black pepper, and milk in a mixing bowl.
4. Grease the same skillet with 1 teaspoon of olive oil and pour the egg mixture into it.
5. Stir cook to make scrambled eggs.
6. Add sausage, mix well and remove the skillet from the heat.
7. Spread an egg roll wrapper on the working surface in a diamond shape position.
8. Add a tablespoon of cheese at the bottom third of the roll wrapper.
9. Top the cheese with egg mixture and wet the edges of the wrapper with water.
10. Fold the two corners of the wrapper and roll it, then seal the edges.
11. Repeat the same steps and divide the rolls in the two crisper plates.
12. Return the crisper plates to the Ninja Foodi Dual Zone Air Fryer.
13. Choose the Air Fry mode for Zone 1 and set the temperature to 375 degrees F and the time to 13 minutes.
14. Select the "MATCH" button to copy the settings for Zone 2.
15. Initiate cooking by pressing the START/STOP button.
16. Flip the rolls after 8 minutes and continue cooking for another 5 minutes.
17. Serve warm and fresh.

Nutrition:

- (Per serving) Calories 282 | Fat 15g |Sodium 526mg | Carbs 20g | Fiber 0.6g | Sugar 3.3g | Protein 16g

Onion Omelette And Buffalo Egg Cups

Servings: 4
Cooking Time: 15 Minutes

Ingredients:

- Onion Omelette:
- 3 eggs
- Salt and ground black pepper, to taste
- ½ teaspoons soy sauce
- 1 large onion, chopped
- 2 tablespoons grated Cheddar cheese
- Cooking spray
- Buffalo Egg Cups:
- 4 large eggs
- 60 g full-fat cream cheese
- 2 tablespoons buffalo sauce
- 120 ml shredded sharp Cheddar cheese

Directions:

1. Make the Onion Omelette :
2. Preheat the zone 1 air fryer drawer to 180°C.
3. In a bowl, whisk together the eggs, salt, pepper, and soy sauce.
4. Spritz a small pan with cooking spray. Spread the chopped onion across the bottom of the pan, then transfer the pan to the zone 1 air fryer drawer.
5. Bake in the preheated air fryer for 6 minutes or until the onion is translucent.
6. Add the egg mixture on top of the onions to coat well. Add the cheese on top, then continue baking for another 6 minutes.
7. Allow to cool before serving.
8. Make the Buffalo Egg Cups :
9. Crack eggs into two ramekins.
10. In a small microwave-safe bowl, mix cream cheese, buffalo sauce, and Cheddar. Microwave for 20 seconds and then stir. Place a spoonful into each ramekin on top of the eggs.
11. Place ramekins into the zone 2 air fryer drawer.
12. Adjust the temperature to 160°C and bake for 15 minutes.
13. Serve warm.

Healthy Oatmeal Muffins

Servings: 6

Cooking Time: 17 Minutes

Ingredients:

- 1 egg
- ¼ tsp ground ginger
- 1 tsp ground cinnamon
- ½ tsp baking soda
- ½ tsp baking powder
- 55g brown sugar
- ½ tsp vanilla
- 2 tbsp butter, melted
- 125g applesauce
- 61ml milk
- 68gm whole wheat flour
- 100gm quick oats
- Pinch of salt

Directions:

1. In a mixing bowl, mix together all dry the ingredients.
2. In a separate bowl, add the remaining ingredients and mix well.
3. Add the dry ingredients mixture into the wet mixture and mix until well combined.
4. Pour the batter into the silicone muffin moulds.
5. Insert a crisper plate in the Ninja Foodi air fryer baskets.
6. Place muffin moulds in both baskets.
7. Select zone 1 then select "bake" mode and set the temperature to 390 degrees F for 17 minutes. Press "start/stop" to begin.

Nutrition:

- (Per serving) Calories 173 | Fat 5.8g |Sodium 177mg | Carbs 26.6g | Fiber 2.1g | Sugar 8.7g | Protein 4.2g

Crispy Hash Browns

Servings: 4

Cooking Time: 13 Minutes.

Ingredients:

- 3 russet potatoes
- ¼ cup chopped green peppers
- ¼ cup chopped red peppers
- ¼ cup chopped onions
- 2 garlic cloves chopped
- 1 teaspoon paprika
- Salt and black pepper, to taste
- 2 teaspoons olive oil

Directions:

1. Peel and grate all the potatoes with the help of a cheese grater.
2. Add potato shreds to a bowl filled with cold water and leave it soaked for 25 minutes.
3. Drain the water and place the potato shreds on a plate lined with a paper towel.
4. Transfer the shreds to a dry bowl and add olive oil, paprika, garlic, and black pepper.
5. Make four flat patties out of the potato mixture and place two into each of the crisper plate.
6. Return the crisper plate to the Ninja Foodi Dual Zone Air Fryer.
7. Choose the Air Fry mode for Zone 1 and set the temperature to 390 degrees F and set the time to 13 minutes.
8. Select the "MATCH" button to copy the settings for Zone 2.
9. Initiate cooking by pressing the START/STOP button.
10. Flip the potato hash browns once cooked halfway through, then resume cooking.
11. Once done, serve warm.

Nutrition:

- (Per serving) Calories 190 | Fat 18g |Sodium 150mg | Carbs 0.6g | Fiber 0.4g | Sugar 0.4g | Protein 7.2g

Egg And Bacon Muffins

Servings: 1

Cooking Time: 15 Minutes

Ingredients:

- 2 eggs
- Salt and ground black pepper, to taste
- 1 tablespoon green pesto
- 85 g shredded Cheddar cheese
- 140 g cooked bacon
- 1 spring onion, chopped

Directions:

1. Line a cupcake tin with parchment paper. Beat the eggs with pepper, salt, and pesto in a bowl. Mix in the cheese.
2. Pour the eggs into the cupcake tin and top with the bacon and spring onion.
3. Place the cupcake tin into the zone 1 drawer and bake at 180°C for 15 minutes, or until the egg is set. Serve immediately.

Cinnamon Apple French Toast

Servings: 8
Cooking Time: 10 Minutes

Ingredients:

- 1 egg, lightly beaten
- 4 bread slices
- 1 tbsp cinnamon
- 15ml milk
- 23ml maple syrup
- 45 ml applesauce

Directions:

1. In a bowl, whisk egg, milk, cinnamon, applesauce, and maple syrup.
2. Insert a crisper plate in the Ninja Foodi air fryer baskets.
3. Dip each slice in egg mixture and place in both baskets.
4. Select zone 1 then select "air fry" mode and set the temperature to 355 degrees F for 10 minutes. Press "match" to match zone 2 settings to zone 1. Press "start/stop" to begin.

Nutrition:

- (Per serving) Calories 64 | Fat 1.5g |Sodium 79mg | Carbs 10.8g | Fiber 1.3g | Sugar 4.8g | Protein 2.3g

Mozzarella Bacon Calzones

Servings: 4
Cooking Time: 12 Minutes

Ingredients:

- 2 large eggs
- 235 ml blanched finely ground almond flour
- 475 ml shredded Mozzarella cheese
- 60 g cream cheese, softened and broken into small pieces
- 4 slices cooked bacon, crumbled

Directions:

1. Beat eggs in a small bowl. Pour into a medium nonstick skillet over medium heat and scramble. Set aside.
2. In a large microwave-safe bowl, mix flour and Mozzarella. Add cream cheese to the bowl.
3. Place bowl in microwave and cook 45 seconds on high to melt cheese, then stir with a fork until a soft dough ball forms.
4. Cut a piece of parchment to fit air fryer drawer. Separate dough into two sections and press each out into an 8-inch round.
5. On half of each dough round, place half of the scrambled eggs and crumbled bacon. Fold the other side of the dough over and press to seal the edges.
6. Place calzones on ungreased parchment and into the zone 1 air fryer drawer. Adjust the temperature to 176°C and set the timer for 12 minutes, turning calzones halfway through cooking. Crust will be golden and firm when done.
7. Let calzones cool on a cooking rack 5 minutes before serving.

Turkey Ham Muffins

Servings: 16
Cooking Time: 10 Minutes

Ingredients:

- 1 egg
- 340g all-purpose flour
- 85g turkey ham, chopped
- 2 tbsp mix herbs, chopped
- 235g cheddar cheese, shredded
- 1 onion, chopped
- 2 tsp baking powder
- 2 tbsp butter, melted
- 237ml milk
- Pepper
- Salt

Directions:

1. In a large bowl, mix flour and baking powder.
2. Add egg, butter, and milk and mix until well combined.
3. Add herbs, cheese, onion, and turkey ham and mix well.
4. Insert a crisper plate in the Ninja Foodi air fryer baskets.
5. Pour the batter into the silicone muffin moulds.
6. Place muffin moulds in both baskets.
7. Select zone 1, then select "air fry" mode and set the temperature to 355 degrees F for 10 minutes. Press "match" to match zone 2 settings to zone 1. Press "start/stop" to begin.

Nutrition:

- (Per serving) Calories 140 | Fat 4.8g |Sodium 126mg | Carbs 18.2g | Fiber 0.7g | Sugar 1.2g | Protein 5.8g

Breakfast Meatballs

Servings: 18 Meatballs
Cooking Time: 15 Minutes
Ingredients:

- 450 g pork sausage meat, removed from casings
- ½ teaspoon salt
- ¼ teaspoon ground black pepper
- 120 ml shredded sharp Cheddar cheese
- 30 g cream cheese, softened
- 1 large egg, whisked

Directions:

1. Combine all ingredients in a large bowl. Form mixture into eighteen 1-inch meatballs.
2. Place meatballs into the two ungreased air fryer drawers. Adjust the temperature to 204°C and air fry for 15 minutes, shaking drawers three times during cooking. Meatballs will be browned on the outside and have an internal temperature of at least 64°C when completely cooked. Serve warm.

Baked Eggs

Servings: 10
Cooking Time: 12 Minutes
Ingredients:

- 450g marinara sauce, divided
- 2 tablespoons capers, drained and divided
- 16 eggs
- 120g whipping cream, divided
- 50g Parmesan cheese, shredded and divided
- Salt and ground black pepper, as required

Directions:

1. Press "Zone 1" and "Zone 2" and then rotate the knob to select "Bake".
2. Set the temperature to 200 degrees C and then set the time for 5 minutes to preheat.
3. Divide the marinara sauce in the bottom of 8 greased ramekins evenly and top with capers.
4. Carefully crack 2 eggs over marinara sauce into each ramekin and top with cream, followed by the Parmesan cheese.
5. Sprinkle each ramekin with salt and black pepper.
6. After preheating, arrange the ramekins into the basket of each zone.
7. Slide the basket into the Air Fryer and set the time for 12 minutes.
8. After cooking time is completed, remove the ramekins from Air Fryer.
9. Serve hot.

Sweet Potato Hash

Servings: 4
Cooking Time: 15 Minutes
Ingredients:

- 3 sweet potatoes, peel & cut into ½-inch pieces
- ½ tsp cinnamon
- 2 tbsp olive oil
- 1 bell pepper, cut into ½-inch pieces
- ½ tsp dried thyme
- ½ tsp nutmeg
- 1 medium onion, cut into ½-inch pieces
- Pepper
- Salt

Directions:

1. In a bowl, toss sweet potatoes with the remaining ingredients.
2. Insert a crisper plate in Ninja Foodi air fryer baskets.
3. Add potato mixture in both baskets.
4. Select zone 1 then select "air fry" mode and set the temperature to 355 degrees F for 15 minutes. Press "match" to match zone 2 settings to zone 1. Press "start/stop" to begin.

Nutrition:

- (Per serving) Calories 167 | Fat 7.3g |Sodium 94mg | Carbs 24.9g | Fiber 4.2g | Sugar 6.8g | Protein 2.2g

Sausage & Butternut Squash

Servings: 2
Cooking Time: 20 Minutes
Ingredients:

- 450g butternut squash, diced
- 70g kielbasa, diced
- ¼ onion, diced
- ¼ tsp garlic powder
- ½ tbsp olive oil
- Pepper
- Salt

Directions:

1. In a bowl, toss butternut squash with garlic powder, oil, onion, kielbasa, pepper, and salt.
2. Insert a crisper plate in the Ninja Foodi air fryer baskets.
3. Add sausage and butternut squash mixture in both baskets.
4. Select zone 1, then select "air fry" mode and set the temperature to 375 degrees F for 20 minutes. Press "match" to match zone 2 settings to zone 1. Press "start/stop" to begin. Stir halfway through.

Nutrition:

- (Per serving) Calories 68 | Fat 3.6g |Sodium 81mg | Carbs 9.7g | Fiber 1.7g | Sugar 2.2g | Protein 0.9g

Air Fried Bacon And Eggs

Servings: 1

Cooking Time: 10 Minutes

Ingredients:

- 2 eggs
- 2 slices bacon

Directions:

1. Grease a ramekin using cooking spray.
2. Install the crisper plate in the zone 1 drawer and place the bacon inside it. Insert the drawer into the unit.
3. Crack the eggs and add them to the greased ramekin.
4. Install the crisper plate in the zone 2 drawer and place the ramekin inside it. Insert the drawer into the unit.
5. Select zone 1 to AIR FRY for 9–11 minutes at 400 degrees F/ 200 degrees C. Select zone 2 to AIR FRY for 8–9 minutes at 350 degrees F/ 175 degrees C. Press SYNC.
6. Press START/STOP to begin cooking.
7. Enjoy!

Nutrition:

- (Per serving) Calories 331 | Fat 24.5g | Sodium 1001mg | Carbs 1.2g | Fiber 0g | Sugar 0.7g | Protein 25.3g

Honey Banana Oatmeal

Servings: 4

Cooking Time: 8 Minutes

Ingredients:

- 2 eggs
- 2 tbsp honey
- 1 tsp vanilla
- 45g quick oats
- 73ml milk
- 30g Greek yoghurt
- 219g banana, mashed

Directions:

1. In a bowl, mix eggs, milk, yoghurt, honey, vanilla, oats, and mashed banana until well combined.
2. Pour batter into the four greased ramekins.
3. Insert a crisper plate in the Ninja Foodi air fryer baskets.
4. Place ramekins in both baskets.
5. Select zone 1 then select “air fry” mode and set the temperature to 390 degrees F for 8 minutes. Press “match” to match zone 2 settings to zone 1. Press “start/stop” to begin.

Nutrition:

- (Per serving) Calories 228 | Fat 4.6g |Sodium 42mg | Carbs 40.4g | Fiber 4.2g | Sugar 16.1g | Protein 7.7g

Red Pepper And Feta Frittata And Bacon Eggs On The Go

Servings: 5

Cooking Time: 20 Minutes

Ingredients:

- Red Pepper and Feta Frittata:
- Olive oil cooking spray
- 8 large eggs
- 1 medium red pepper, diced
- ½ teaspoon salt
- ½ teaspoon black pepper
- 1 garlic clove, minced
- 120 ml feta, divided
- Bacon Eggs on the Go:
- 2 eggs
- 110 g bacon, cooked
- Salt and ground black pepper, to taste

Directions:

1. Make the Red Pepper and Feta Frittata :
2. Preheat the air fryer to 180°C. Lightly coat the inside of a 6-inch round cake pan with olive oil cooking spray.
3. In a large bowl, beat the eggs for 1 to 2 minutes, or until well combined.
4. Add the red pepper, salt, black pepper, and garlic to the eggs, and mix together until the red pepper is distributed throughout.
5. Fold in 60 ml the feta cheese.
6. Pour the egg mixture into the prepared cake pan, and sprinkle the remaining 60 ml feta over the top.
7. Place into the zone 1 air fryer basket and bake for 18 to 20 minutes, or until the eggs are set in the center.
8. Remove from the air fryer and allow to cool for 5 minutes before serving.
9. Make the Bacon Eggs on the Go :
10. Preheat the air fryer to 205°C. Put liners in a regular cupcake tin.
11. Crack an egg into each of the cups and add the bacon. Season with some pepper and salt.
12. Bake in the preheated zone 2 air fryer basket for 15 minutes, or until the eggs are set. Serve warm.

Brussels Sprouts Potato Hash

Servings: 4
Cooking Time: 10 Minutes

Ingredients:

- 455g Brussels sprouts
- 1 small to medium red onion
- 227g baby red potatoes
- 2 tablespoons avocado oil
- ½ teaspoon salt
- ½ teaspoon black pepper

Directions:

1. Peel and boil potatoes in salted water for 15 minutes until soft.
2. Drain and allow them to cool down then dice.
3. Shred Brussels sprouts and toss them with potatoes and the rest of the ingredients.
4. Divide this veggies hash mixture in both of the air fryer baskets.
5. Return the air fryer basket 1 to Zone 1, and basket 2 to Zone 2 of the Ninja Foodi 2-Basket Air Fryer.
6. Choose the "Air Fry" mode for Zone 1 with 375 degrees F temperature and 10 minutes of cooking time.
7. Select the "MATCH COOK" option to copy the settings for Zone 2.
8. Initiate cooking by pressing the START/PAUSE BUTTON.
9. Shake the veggies once cooked halfway through.
10. Serve warm.

Nutrition:

- (Per serving) Calories 305 | Fat 25g |Sodium 532mg | Carbs 2.3g | Fiber 0.4g | Sugar 2g | Protein 18.3g

Eggs In Avocado Cups

Servings: 4
Cooking Time: 12 Minutes

Ingredients:

- 2 avocados, halved and pitted
- 4 eggs
- Salt and ground black pepper, as required

Directions:

1. Line either basket of "Zone 1" and "Zone 2" of Ninja Foodi 2-Basket Air Fryer with a greased square piece of foil.
2. Press your chosen zone - "Zone 1" and "Zone 2" and then rotate the knob to select "Bake".
3. Set the temperature to 200 degrees C and then set the time for 5 minutes to preheat.
4. Meanwhile, carefully scoop out about 2 teaspoons of flesh from each avocado half.
5. Crack 1 egg in each avocado half and sprinkle with salt and black pepper.
6. After preheating, arrange 2 avocado halves into the basket.
7. Slide the basket into the Air Fryer and set the time for 12 minutes.
8. After cooking time is completed, transfer the avocado halves and onto serving plates and serve hot.

Honey-apricot Granola With Greek Yoghurt

Servings: 6
Cooking Time: 30 Minutes

Ingredients:

- 235 ml rolled oats
- 60 ml dried apricots, diced
- 60 ml almond slivers
- 60 ml walnuts, chopped
- 60 ml pumpkin seeds
- 60 to 80 ml honey, plus more for drizzling
- 1 tablespoon olive oil
- 1 teaspoon ground cinnamon
- ¼ teaspoon ground nutmeg
- ¼ teaspoon salt
- 2 tablespoons sugar-free dark chocolate chips (optional)
- 700 ml fat-free plain Greek yoghurt

Directions:

1. Line the zone 1 and zone 2 drawer with two parchment papers. In a large bowl, combine the oats, apricots, almonds, walnuts, pumpkin seeds, honey, olive oil, cinnamon, nutmeg, and salt, mixing so that the honey, oil, and spices are well distributed. Pour the mixture onto the parchment papers and spread it into an even layer.
2. Bake at 130°C for 10 minutes, then shake or stir and spread back out into an even layer. Continue baking for 10 minutes more, then repeat the process of shaking or stirring the mixture.
3. Bake for an additional 10 minutes before removing from the air fryer. Allow the granola to cool completely before stirring in the chocolate chips and pouring into an airtight container for storage. For each serving, top 120 ml Greek yoghurt with 80 ml granola and a drizzle of honey, if needed.

Asparagus And Bell Pepper Strata And Greek Bagels

Servings: 6

Cooking Time: 14 To 20 Minutes

Ingredients:

- Asparagus and Bell Pepper Strata:
- 8 large asparagus spears, trimmed and cut into 2-inch pieces
- 80 ml shredded carrot
- 120 ml chopped red pepper
- 2 slices wholemeal bread, cut into ½-inch cubes
- 3 egg whites
- 1 egg
- 3 tablespoons 1% milk
- ½ teaspoon dried thyme
- Greek Bagels:
- 120 ml self-raising flour, plus more for dusting
- 120 ml plain Greek yoghurt
- 1 egg
- 1 tablespoon water
- 4 teaspoons sesame seeds or za'atar
- Cooking oil spray
- 1 tablespoon butter, melted

Directions:

1. Make the Asparagus and Bell Pepper Strata :
2. In a baking pan, combine the asparagus, carrot, red bell pepper, and 1 tablespoon of water. Bake in the air fryer at 166°C for 3 to 5 minutes, or until crisp-tender. Drain well.
3. Add the bread cubes to the vegetables and gently toss.
4. In a medium bowl, whisk the egg whites, egg, milk, and thyme until frothy.
5. Pour the egg mixture into the pan. Bake in the zone 1 drawer for 11 to 15 minutes, or until the strata is slightly puffy and set and the top starts to brown. Serve.
6. Make the Greek Bagels :
7. In a large bowl, using a wooden spoon, stir together the flour and yoghurt until a tacky dough forms. Transfer the dough to a lightly floured work surface and roll the dough into a ball.
8. Cut the dough into 2 pieces and roll each piece into a log. Form each log into a bagel shape, pinching the ends together.
9. In a small bowl, whisk the egg and water. Brush the egg wash on the bagels.
10. Sprinkle 2 teaspoons of the toppings on each bagel and gently press it into the dough.
11. Insert the crisper plate into the zone 2 drawer and the drawer into the unit. Preheat the drawer by selecting BAKE, setting the temperature to 166°C, and setting the time to 3 minutes. Select START/STOP to begin.
12. Once the drawer is preheated, spray the crisper plate with cooking spray. Drizzle the bagels with the butter and place them into the drawer.
13. Select BAKE, set the temperature to 166°C, and set the time to 10 minutes. Select START/STOP to begin.
14. When the cooking is complete, the bagels should be lightly golden on the outside. Serve warm.

Yellow Potatoes With Eggs

Servings:2

Cooking Time:35

Ingredients:

- 1 pound of Dutch yellow potatoes, quartered
- 1 red bell pepper, chopped
- Salt and black pepper, to taste
- 1 green bell pepper, chopped
- 2 teaspoons of olive oil
- 2 teaspoons of garlic powder
- 1 teaspoon of onion powder
- 1 egg
- ¼ teaspoon of butter

Directions:

1. Toss together diced potatoes, green pepper, red pepper, salt, black pepper, and olive oil along with garlic powder and onion powder.
2. Put in the zone 1 basket of the air fryer.
3. Take ramekin and grease it with oil spray.
4. Whisk egg in a bowl and add salt and pepper along with ½ teaspoon of butter.
5. Pour egg into a ramekin and place it in a zone 2 basket.
6. Now start cooking and set a timer for zone 1 basket to 30-35 minutes at 400 degrees at AIR FRY mode.
7. Now for zone 2, set it on AIR FRY mode at 350 degrees F for 8-10 minutes.
8. Press the Smart finish button and press start, it will finish both at the same time.
9. Once done, serve and enjoy.

Nutrition:

- (Per serving) Calories252 | Fat7.5g | Sodium 37mg | Carbs 40g | Fiber3.9g | Sugar 7g | Protein 6.7g

Spinach And Red Pepper Egg Cups With Coffee-glazed Canadian Bacon

Servings:6
Cooking Time: 13 Minutes
Ingredients:

- FOR THE EGG CUPS
- 4 large eggs
- ¼ cup heavy (whipping) cream
- ¼ teaspoon kosher salt
- ¼ teaspoon freshly ground black pepper
- ½ cup roasted red peppers (about 1 whole pepper), drained and chopped
- ½ cup baby spinach, chopped
- FOR THE CANADIAN BACON
- ¼ cup brewed coffee
- 2 tablespoons maple syrup
- 1 tablespoon light brown sugar
- 6 slices Canadian bacon

Directions:

1. To prep the egg cups: In a medium bowl, whisk together the eggs and cream until well combined with a uniform, light color. Stir in the salt, black pepper, roasted red peppers, and spinach until combined.
2. Divide the egg mixture among 6 silicone muffin cups.
3. To prep the Canadian bacon: In a small bowl, whisk together the coffee, maple syrup, and brown sugar.
4. Using a basting brush, brush the glaze onto both sides of each slice of bacon.
5. To cook the egg cups and Canadian bacon: Install a crisper plate in each of the two baskets. Place the egg cups in the Zone 1 basket and insert the basket in the unit. Place the glazed bacon in the Zone 2 basket, making sure the slices don't overlap, and insert the basket in the unit. It is okay if the bacon overlaps a little bit.
6. Select Zone 1, select BAKE, set the temperature to 325°F, and set the time to 13 minutes.
7. Select Zone 2, select AIR FRY, set the temperature to 400°F, and set the time to 5 minutes. Select SMART FINISH.
8. Press START/PAUSE to begin cooking.
9. When the Zone 2 timer reads 2 minutes, press START/PAUSE. Remove the basket and use silicone-tipped tongs to flip the bacon. Reinsert the basket and press START/PAUSE to resume cooking.
10. When cooking is complete, serve the egg cups with the Canadian bacon.

Nutrition:

- (Per serving) Calories: 180; Total fat: 9.5g; Saturated fat: 4.5g; Carbohydrates: 9g; Fiber: 0g; Protein: 14g; Sodium: 688mg

Cinnamon Air Fryer Apples

Servings: 4
Cooking Time: 15 Minutes
Ingredients:

- 2 apples, cut in half and cored
- 2 tablespoons butter, melted
- 40g oats
- 3 teaspoons honey
- ½ teaspoon ground cinnamon

Directions:

1. Apply the butter to the apple halves' tops.
2. Combine the remaining butter, oats, honey, and cinnamon in a mixing bowl.
3. Distribute the mixture evenly over the apples' tops.
4. Press either "Zone 1" or "Zone 2" and then rotate the knob to select "Air Fryer".
5. Set the temperature to 190 degrees C, and then set the time for 3 minutes to preheat.
6. After preheating, Arrange the apples in the basket.
7. Slide basket into Air Fryer and set the time for 15 minutes.
8. After cooking time is completed, remove basket from Air Fryer.
9. Place them on serving plates and serve.

Breakfast Sausage And Cauliflower

Servings: 4
Cooking Time: 45 Minutes
Ingredients:

- 450 g sausage meat, cooked and crumbled
- 475 ml double/whipping cream
- 1 head cauliflower, chopped
- 235 ml grated Cheddar cheese, plus more for topping
- 8 eggs, beaten
- Salt and ground black pepper, to taste

Directions:

1. Preheat the air fryer to 176°C.
2. In a large bowl, mix the sausage, cream, chopped cauliflower, cheese and eggs. Sprinkle with salt and ground black pepper.
3. Pour the mixture into a greased casserole dish. Bake in the preheated air fryer for 45 minutes or until firm.
4. Top with more Cheddar cheese and serve.

Air Fryer Sausage Patties

Servings: 12

Cooking Time: 10 Minutes

Ingredients:

- 1-pound pork sausage or ready-made patties
- Fennel seeds or preferred seasonings

Directions:

1. Prepare the sausage by slicing it into patties, then flavor it with fennel seed or your favorite seasonings.
2. Install a crisper plate in both drawers. Place half the patties in zone 1 and half in zone 2, then insert the drawers into the unit.
3. Select zone 1, select AIR FRY, set temperature to 390 degrees F/ 200 degrees C, and set time to 10 minutes.
4. Select MATCH to match zone 2 settings to zone 1.
5. Press the START/STOP button to begin cooking.
6. When cooking is complete, remove the patties from the unit and serve with sauce or make a burger.

Nutrition:

- (Per serving) Calories 130 | Fat 10.5g | Sodium 284mg | Carbs 0.3g | Fiber 0.2g | Sugar 0g | Protein 7.4g

Bacon And Egg Omelet

Servings:2

Cooking Time:10

Ingredients:

- 2 eggs, whisked
- ½ teaspoon of chopped tomatoes
- Sea Salt and black pepper, to taste
- 2 teaspoons of almond milk
- 1 teaspoon of cilantro, chopped
- 1 small green chili, chopped
- 4 slices of bacon

Directions:

1. Take a bowl and whisk eggs in it.
2. Then add green chili salt, black pepper, cilantro, almond milk, and chopped tomatoes.
3. Oil greases the ramekins.
4. Pour this into ramekins.
5. Put the bacon in the zone 1 basket and ramekins in zone 2 basket of the Ninja Foodie 2-Basket Air Fryer.
6. Now for zone 1, set it to AIR FRY mode at 400 degrees F for 10 minutes
7. And for zone 2, set it 350 degrees for 10 minutes in AIR FRY mode.
8. Press the Smart finish button and press start, it will finish both at the same time.
9. Once done, serve and enjoy.

Nutrition:

- (Per serving) Calories 285| Fat 21.5g| Sodium1000 mg | Carbs 2.2g | Fiber 0.1g| Sugar1 g | Protein 19.7g

Spinach And Swiss Frittata With Mushrooms

Servings: 4

Cooking Time: 20 Minutes

Ingredients:

- Olive oil cooking spray
- 8 large eggs
- ½ teaspoon salt
- ½ teaspoon black pepper
- 1 garlic clove, minced
- 475 ml fresh baby spinach
- 110 g baby mushrooms, sliced
- 1 shallot, diced
- 120 ml shredded Swiss cheese, divided
- Hot sauce, for serving (optional)

Directions:

1. Lightly coat the inside of a 6-inch round cake pan with olive oil cooking spray. In a large bowl, beat the eggs, salt, pepper, and garlic for 1 to 2 minutes, or until well combined.
2. Fold in the spinach, mushrooms, shallot, and 60 ml the Swiss cheese. Pour the egg mixture into the prepared cake pan, and sprinkle the remaining 60 ml Swiss over the top. Place into the zone 1 drawer.
3. Select Bake button and adjust temperature to 180°C, set time to 18 to 20 minutes and press Start. After the end, remove from the air fryer and allow to cool for 5 minutes. Drizzle with hot sauce before serving.

Chicken Stuffed Mushrooms

Servings: 6
Cooking Time: 15 Minutes.

Ingredients:

- 6 large fresh mushrooms, stems removed
- Stuffing:
- ½ cup chicken meat, cubed
- 1 (4 ounces) package cream cheese, softened
- ¼ lb. imitation crabmeat, flaked
- 1 cup butter
- 1 garlic clove, peeled and minced
- Black pepper and salt to taste
- Garlic powder to taste
- Crushed red pepper to taste

Directions:

1. Melt and heat butter in a skillet over medium heat.
2. Add chicken and sauté for 5 minutes.
3. Add in all the remaining ingredients for the stuffing.
4. Cook for 5 minutes, then turn off the heat.
5. Allow the mixture to cool. Stuff each mushroom with a tablespoon of this mixture.
6. Divide the stuffed mushrooms in the two crisper plates.
7. Return the crisper plate to the Ninja Foodi Dual Zone Air Fryer.
8. Choose the Air Fry mode for Zone 1 and set the temperature to 375 degrees F and the time to 15 minutes.
9. Select the "MATCH" button to copy the settings for Zone 2.
10. Initiate cooking by pressing the START/STOP button.
11. Serve warm.

Nutrition:

- (Per serving) Calories 180 | Fat 3.2g |Sodium 133mg | Carbs 32g | Fiber 1.1g | Sugar 1.8g | Protein 9g

Parmesan Crush Chicken

Servings:4
Cooking Time:18

Ingredients:

- 4 chicken breasts
- 1 cup parmesan cheese
- 1 cup bread crumb
- 2 eggs, whisked
- Salt, to taste
- Oil spray, for greasing

Directions:

1. Whisk egg in a large bowl and set aside.
2. Season the chicken breast with salt and then put it in egg wash.
3. Next, dredge it in breadcrumb then parmesan cheese.
4. Line both the basket of the air fryer with parchment paper.
5. Divided the breast pieces between the backsets, and oil spray the breast pieces.
6. Set zone 1 basket to air fry mode at 350 degrees F for 18 minutes.
7. Select the MATCH button for the zone 2 basket.
8. Once it's done, serve.

Nutrition:

- (Per serving) Calories574 | Fat25g | Sodium848 mg | Carbs 21.4g | Fiber 1.2g| Sugar 1.8g | Protein 64.4g

Kale Potato Nuggets

Servings: 4
Cooking Time: 15 Minutes

Ingredients:

- 279g potatoes, chopped, boiled & mashed
- 268g kale, chopped
- 1 garlic clove, minced
- 30ml milk
- Pepper
- Salt

Directions:

1. In a bowl, mix potatoes, kale, milk, garlic, pepper, and salt until well combined.
2. Insert a crisper plate in the Ninja Foodi air fryer baskets.
3. Make small balls from the potato mixture and place them both baskets.
4. Select zone 1 then select "air fry" mode and set the temperature to 390 degrees F for 15 minutes. Press "match" to match zone 2 settings to zone 1. Press "start/stop" to begin. Turn halfway through.

Crab Rangoon Dip With Crispy Wonton Strips

Servings:6

Cooking Time: 15 Minutes

Ingredients:

- FOR THE DIP
- 1 (6-ounce) can pink crab, drained
- 8 ounces (16 tablespoons) cream cheese, at room temperature
- ½ cup sour cream
- 1 tablespoon chopped scallions
- ½ teaspoon garlic powder
- 1 teaspoon Worcestershire sauce
- ¼ teaspoon kosher salt
- 1 cup shredded part-skim mozzarella cheese
- FOR THE WONTON STRIPS
- 12 wonton wrappers
- 1 tablespoon olive oil
- ¼ teaspoon kosher salt

Directions:

1. To prep the dip: In a medium bowl, mix the crab, cream cheese, sour cream, scallions, garlic powder, Worcestershire sauce, and salt until smooth.
2. To prep the wonton strips: Brush both sides of the wonton wrappers with the oil and sprinkle with salt. Cut the wonton wrappers into ¾-inch-wide strips.
3. To cook the dip and strips: Pour the dip into the Zone 1 basket, top with the mozzarella cheese, and insert the basket in the unit. Install a crisper plate in the Zone 2 basket, add the wonton strips, and insert the basket in the unit.
4. Select Zone 1, select BAKE, set the temperature to 330°F, and set the time to 15 minutes.
5. Select Zone 2, select AIR FRY, set the temperature to 350°F, and set the time to 6 minutes. Select SMART FINISH.
6. Press START/PAUSE to begin cooking.
7. When the Zone 2 timer reads 4 minutes, press START/PAUSE. Remove the basket and shake well to redistribute the wonton strips. Reinsert the basket and press START/PAUSE to resume cooking.
8. When the Zone 2 timer reads 2 minutes, press START/PAUSE. Remove the basket and shake well to redistribute the wonton strips. Reinsert the basket and press START/PAUSE to resume cooking.
9. When cooking is complete, the dip will be bubbling and golden brown on top and the wonton strips will be crunchy. Serve warm.

Nutrition:

- (Per serving) Calories: 315; Total fat: 23g; Saturated fat: 12g; Carbohydrates: 14g; Fiber: 0.5g; Protein: 14g; Sodium: 580mg

Shrimp Pirogues

Servings: 8

Cooking Time: 4 To 5 Minutes

Ingredients:

- 340 g small, peeled, and deveined raw shrimp
- 85 g soft white cheese, room temperature
- 2 tablespoons natural yoghurt
- 1 teaspoon lemon juice
- 1 teaspoon dried dill weed, crushed
- Salt, to taste
- 4 small hothouse cucumbers, each approximately 6 inches long

Directions:

1. Pour 4 tablespoons water in bottom of air fryer drawer.
2. Place shrimp in air fryer basket in single layer and air fry at 200°C for 4 to 5 minutes, just until done. Watch carefully because shrimp cooks quickly, and overcooking makes it tough.
3. Chop shrimp into small pieces, no larger than ½ inch. Refrigerate while mixing the remaining ingredients.
4. With a fork, mash and whip the soft white cheese until smooth.
5. Stir in the yoghurt and beat until smooth. Stir in lemon juice, dill weed, and chopped shrimp.
6. Taste for seasoning. If needed, add ¼ to ½ teaspoon salt to suit your taste.
7. Store in refrigerator until serving time.
8. When ready to serve, wash and dry cucumbers and split them lengthwise. Scoop out the seeds and turn cucumbers upside down on paper towels to drain for 10 minutes.
9. Just before filling, wipe centres of cucumbers dry. Spoon the shrimp mixture into the pirogues and cut in half crosswise. Serve immediately.

Caramelized Onion Dip With White Cheese

Servings: 8 To 10
Cooking Time: 30 Minutes

Ingredients:

- 1 tablespoon butter
- 1 medium onion, halved and thinly sliced
- ¼ teaspoon rock salt, plus additional for seasoning
- 113 g soft white cheese
- 120 ml sour cream
- ¼ teaspoon onion powder
- 1 tablespoon chopped fresh chives
- Black pepper, to taste
- Thick-cut potato crisps or vegetable crisps

Directions:

1. Place the butter in a baking pan. Place the pan in the zone 1 air fryer basket. Set the air fryer to 90°C for 1 minute, or until the butter is melted. Add the onions and salt to the pan.
2. Set the air fryer to 90°C for 15 minutes, or until onions are softened. Set the air fryer to 190°C for 15 minutes, until onions are a deep golden brown, stirring two or three times during the cooking time. Let cool completely.
3. In a medium bowl, stir together the cooked onions, soft white cheese, sour cream, onion powder, and chives. Season with salt and pepper. Cover and refrigerate for 2 hours to allow the flavours to blend.
4. Serve the dip with potato crisps or vegetable crisps.

Tater Tots

Servings: 4
Cooking Time: 8 Minutes

Ingredients:

- 16 ounces tater tots
- ½ cup shredded cheddar cheese
- 1½ teaspoons bacon bits
- 2 green onions, chopped
- Sour cream (optional)

Directions:

1. Place a crisper plate in each drawer. Put the tater tots into the drawers in a single layer. Insert the drawers into the unit.
2. Select zone 1, then AIR FRY, then set the temperature to 360 degrees F/ 180 degrees C with a 6-minute timer. To match zone 2 settings to zone 1, choose MATCH. To begin, select START/STOP.
3. When the cooking time is over, add the shredded cheddar cheese, bacon bits, and green onions over the tater tots. Select zone 1, AIR FRY, 360 degrees F/ 180 degrees C, for 4 minutes. Select MATCH. Press START/STOP.
4. Drizzle sour cream over the top before serving.
5. Enjoy!

Nutrition:

- (Per serving) Calories 335 | Fat 19.1g | Sodium 761mg | Carbs 34.1g | Fiber 3g | Sugar 0.6g | Protein 8.9g

Avocado Fries

Servings: 8
Cooking Time: 10 Minutes

Ingredients:

- 60g plain flour
- Salt and ground black pepper, as required
- 2 eggs
- 1 teaspoon water
- 100g seasoned breadcrumbs
- 2 avocados, peeled, pitted and sliced into 8 pieces
- Non-stick cooking spray

Directions:

1. In a shallow bowl, mix together the flour, salt, and black pepper.
2. In a second bowl, add the egg and water and beat well.
3. In a third bowl, place the breadcrumbs.
4. Coat the avocado slices with flour mixture, then dip into egg mixture and finally, coat evenly with the breadcrumbs.
5. Now, spray the avocado slices with cooking spray evenly.
6. Grease one basket of Ninja Foodi 2-Basket Air Fryer.
7. Press either "Zone 1" and "Zone 2" and then rotate the knob to select "Air Fry".
8. Set the temperature to 200 degrees C and then set the time for 5 minutes to preheat.
9. After preheating, arrange the avocado slices into the basket.
10. Slide basket into Air Fryer and set the time for 10 minutes.
11. After cooking time is completed, remove the fries from Air Fryer and serve warm.

Five-ingredient Falafel With Garlic-yoghurt Sauce

Servings: 4
Cooking Time: 15 Minutes

Ingredients:

- Falafel:
- 1 (425 g) can chickpeas, drained and rinsed
- 120 ml fresh parsley
- 2 garlic cloves, minced
- ½ tablespoon ground cumin
- 1 tablespoon wholemeal flour
- Salt
- Garlic-Yoghurt Sauce:
- 240 ml non-fat plain Greek yoghurt
- 1 garlic clove, minced
- 1 tablespoon chopped fresh dill
- 2 tablespoons lemon juice

Directions:

1. Make the Falafel: Preheat the air fryer to 180°C. 2. Put the chickpeas into a food processor. Pulse until mostly chopped, then add the parsley, garlic, and cumin and pulse for another 1 to 2 minutes, or until the ingredients are combined and turning into a dough. 3. Add the flour. Pulse a few more times until combined. The dough will have texture, but the chickpeas should be pulsed into small bits. 4. Using clean hands, roll the dough into 8 balls of equal size, then pat the balls down a bit so they are about ½-thick disks. 5. Spray the zone 1 air fryer basket with olive oil cooking spray, then place the falafel patties in the basket in a single layer, making sure they don't touch each other. 6. Fry in the air fryer for 15 minutes. Make the garlic-yoghurt sauce 7. In a small bowl, combine the yoghurt, garlic, dill, and lemon juice. 8. Once the falafel is done cooking and nicely browned on all sides, remove them from the air fryer and season with salt. 9. Serve hot with a side of dipping sauce.

Beefy Swiss Pastry

Servings: 4
Cooking Time: 10 Minutes

Ingredients:

- 455g of beef mince
- 70g sliced fresh mushrooms
- 80g chopped onion
- 1-½ teaspoons minced garlic
- ¾ teaspoon dried rosemary, crushed
- ¾ teaspoon paprika
- ½ teaspoon salt
- ¼ teaspoon pepper
- 1 sheet frozen puff pastry, thawed
- 151g refrigerated mashed potatoes
- 100g shredded Swiss cheese
- 1 large egg
- 2 tablespoons water

Directions:

1. Cook the beef, mushrooms, and onion in a large frying pan over medium heat until the meat is no longer pink and the veggies are cooked, 8-10 minutes| crumble the meat.
2. Cook for a further minute after adding the garlic. Drain. Season with salt and pepper. Remove the pan from the heat and set it aside.
3. Roll puff pastry into a rectangle on a lightly floured surface. Make four little rectangles out of the dough.
4. Over each square, spread around 2 teaspoons of potatoes. ¾ cup beef mixture on top of each| 25g cheese on each.
5. In a small bowl, whisk together the egg and water| brush the wash over the pastry edges.
6. Bring opposing pastry corners over each bundle and pinch seams together to seal. Brush with the rest of the egg mixture.
7. Press either "Zone 1" or "Zone 2" and then rotate the knob to select "Air Fry".
8. Set the temperature to 190 degrees C, and then set the time for 5 minutes to preheat.
9. After preheating, spray the Air-Fryer basket with cooking spray and line with parchment paper. Arrange pastry in a single layer and spritz them with cooking spray.
10. Slide the basket into the Air Fryer and set the time for 10 minutes.
11. After that, turn them and again cook for 3 minutes longer.
12. After cooking time is completed, transfer them onto serving plates and serve.

Parmesan Wings

Servings: 4
Cooking Time: 30 Minutes

Ingredients:

- 900g chicken wings
- 1 tablespoon olive oil
- 1 tablespoon baking powder
- ½ teaspoon salt
- ½ teaspoon garlic powder
- ½ teaspoon onion powder
- ¼ teaspoon paprika
- ¼ teaspoon black pepper
- 5 tablespoons unsalted butter, melted
- 4-5 cloves garlic, minced
- 25g grated parmesan cheese

Directions:

1. Using paper towels, fully dry the wings and lay them in a large mixing bowl. Toss them in olive oil and toss to coat.
2. Combine the baking powder, salt, garlic powder, onion powder, paprika, and pepper in a small bowl. Toss the wings in the mixture to evenly coat them.
3. Press your chosen zone - "Zone 1" or "Zone 2" and then rotate the knob to select "Air Fry".
4. Set the temperature to 200 degrees C, and then set the time for 5 minutes to preheat.
5. After preheating, spray the Air-Fryer basket of each zone with cooking spray, arrange wings in a single layer, and spritz them with cooking spray.
6. Slide the basket into the Air Fryer and set the time for 15 minutes.
7. Carefully flip the wings and cook for 5 to 8 more minutes.
8. Meanwhile, in a microwave-safe bowl, melt the butter. Combine the minced garlic and parmesan cheese in a mixing bowl.
9. After cooking time is completed, combine with the garlic butter in a large mixing dish and serve on a serving plate.

Mozzarella Sticks

Servings: 6
Cooking Time: 6 Minutes

Ingredients:

- 150g block Mozzarella cheese or string cheese
- 6 slices of white bread
- 1 large egg
- 1 tablespoon water
- 55g panko breadcrumbs
- 1 tablespoon olive oil

Directions:

1. Remove the crust from the bread. Discard or save for breadcrumbs.
2. Roll the bread into thin slices with a rolling pin.
3. Slice mozzarella into 30 cm x 10 cm -long sticks, nearly the same size as your bread slices.
4. In a small bowl, whisk together the egg and the water.
5. Fill a shallow pie plate halfway with panko.
6. Wrap a bread slice around each mozzarella stick.
7. Brush the egg wash around the edge of the bread and push to seal it. Brush all over the bread outside.
8. Dredge in Panko and push to coat on all sides.
9. Line basket with parchment paper.
10. Press either "Zone 1" or "Zone 2" and then rotate the knob to select "Air Fryer".
11. Set the temperature to 200 degrees C, and then set the time for 5 minutes to preheat.
12. After preheating, arrange sticks into the basket.
13. Slide the basket into the Air Fryer and set the time for 6 minutes.
14. After cooking time is completed, place on a wire rack for a few minutes, then transfer onto serving plates and serve.

Bacon-wrapped Shrimp And Jalapeño

Servings: 8
Cooking Time: 26 Minutes

Ingredients:

- 24 large shrimp, peeled and deveined, about 340 g
- 5 tablespoons barbecue sauce, divided
- 12 strips bacon, cut in half
- 24 small pickled jalapeño slices

Directions:

1. Toss together the shrimp and 3 tablespoons of the barbecue sauce. Let stand for 15 minutes. Soak 24 wooden toothpicks in water for 10 minutes. Wrap 1 piece bacon around the shrimp and jalapeño slice, then secure with a toothpick.
2. Preheat the air fryer to 175°C.
3. Place the shrimp in the two air fryer baskets, spacing them ½ inch apart. Air fry for 10 minutes. Turn shrimp over with tongs and air fry for 3 minutes more, or until bacon is golden brown and shrimp are cooked through.
4. Brush with the remaining barbecue sauce and serve.

Parmesan French Fries

Servings: 6
Cooking Time: 20 Minutes.

Ingredients:

- 3 medium russet potatoes
- 2 tablespoons parmesan cheese
- 2 tablespoons fresh parsley, chopped
- 1 tablespoon olive oil
- Salt, to taste

Directions:

1. Wash the potatoes and pass them through the fries' cutter to get ¼-inch-thick fries.
2. Place the fries in a colander and drizzle salt on top.
3. Leave these fries for 10 minutes, then rinse.
4. Toss the potatoes with parmesan cheese, oil, salt, and parsley in a bowl.
5. Divide the potatoes into the two crisper plates.
6. Return the crisper plates to the Ninja Foodi Dual Zone Air Fryer.
7. Choose the Air Fry mode for Zone 1 and set the temperature to 360 degrees F and the time to 20 minutes.
8. Select the "MATCH" button to copy the settings for Zone 2.
9. Initiate cooking by pressing the START/STOP button.
10. Toss the chips once cooked halfway through, then resume cooking.
11. Serve warm.

Nutrition:

- (Per serving) Calories 307 | Fat 8.6g |Sodium 510mg | Carbs 22.2g | Fiber 1.4g | Sugar 13g | Protein 33.6g

Mushroom Rolls

Servings: 10
Cooking Time: 10 Minutes

Ingredients:

- 2 tablespoons olive oil
- 200g large portobello mushrooms, finely chopped
- 1 teaspoon dried oregano
- ½ teaspoon crushed red pepper flakes
- ¼ teaspoon salt
- 200g cream cheese, softened
- 100g whole-milk ricotta cheese
- 10 flour tortillas
- Cooking spray

Directions:

1. Heat the oil in a frying pan over medium heat. Add the mushrooms and cook for 4 minutes.
2. Sauté until mushrooms are browned, about 4-6 minutes, with oregano, pepper flakes, and salt. Cool.
3. Combine the cheeses in a mixing bowl| fold the mushrooms until thoroughly combined. On the bottom centre of each tortilla, spread 3 tablespoons of the mushroom mixture. Tightly roll up and secure with toothpicks.
4. Press either "Zone 1" or "Zone 2" and then rotate the knob to select "Air Fry".
5. Set the temperature to 200 degrees C, and then set the time for 5 minutes to preheat.
6. After preheating, spray the basket with cooking spray and arrange rolls onto basket.
7. Slide the basket into the Air Fryer and set the time for 10 minutes.
8. After cooking time is completed, transfer them onto serving plates and serve.

Fried Okra

Servings: 4
Cooking Time: 10 Minutes

Ingredients:

- 455g fresh okra
- 240ml buttermilk
- 125g plain flour
- 160g polenta
- 1 teaspoon salt
- 1 teaspoon fresh ground pepper

Directions:

1. Wash and trim the ends of the okra before slicing it into 30cm chunks.
2. In a small dish, pour the buttermilk.
3. Combine flour, polenta, salt, and pepper in a separate dish.
4. Coat all sides of okra slices in buttermilk and then in flour mixture.
5. Place a baking sheet on the baskets.
6. Press either "Zone 1" or "Zone 2" and then rotate the knob to select "Air Fryer".
7. Set the temperature to 175 degrees C, and then set the time for 5 minutes to preheat.
8. After preheating, arrange them into the basket.
9. Slide the basket into the Air Fryer and set the time for 8 minutes.
10. After cooking time is completed, place on a wire rack for a few minutes, then transfer onto serving plates and serve.

Pepperoni Pizza Dip

Servings: 6
Cooking Time: 10 Minutes
Ingredients:

- 170 g soft white cheese
- 177 ml shredded Italian cheese blend
- 60 ml sour cream
- 1½ teaspoons dried Italian seasoning
- ¼ teaspoon garlic salt
- ¼ teaspoon onion powder
- 177 ml pizza sauce
- 120 ml sliced miniature pepperoni
- 60 ml sliced black olives
- 1 tablespoon thinly sliced green onion
- Cut-up raw vegetables, toasted baguette slices, pitta chips, or tortilla chips, for serving

Directions:

1. In a small bowl, combine the soft white cheese, 60 ml of the shredded cheese, the sour cream, Italian seasoning, garlic salt, and onion powder. Stir until smooth and the ingredients are well blended.
2. Spread the mixture in a baking pan. Top with the pizza sauce, spreading to the edges. Sprinkle with the remaining 120 ml shredded cheese. Arrange the pepperoni slices on top of the cheese. Top with the black olives and green onion.
3. Place the pan in the zone 1 air fryer basket. Set the air fryer to 175°C for 10 minutes, or until the pepperoni is beginning to brown on the edges and the cheese is bubbly and lightly browned.
4. Let stand for 5 minutes before serving with vegetables, toasted baguette slices, pitta chips, or tortilla chips.

Crispy Filo Artichoke Triangles

Servings: 18 Triangles
Cooking Time: 9 To 12 Minutes
Ingredients:

- 60 ml Ricotta cheese
- 1 egg white
- 80 ml minced and drained artichoke hearts
- 3 tablespoons grated Mozzarella cheese
- ½ teaspoon dried thyme
- 6 sheets frozen filo pastry, thawed
- 2 tablespoons melted butter

Directions:

1. Preheat the air fryer to 205°C.
2. In a small bowl, combine the Ricotta cheese, egg white, artichoke hearts, Mozzarella cheese, and thyme, and mix well.
3. Cover the filo pastry with a damp kitchen towel while you work so it doesn't dry out. Using one sheet at a time, place on the work surface and cut into thirds lengthwise.
4. Put about 1½ teaspoons of the filling on each strip at the base. Fold the bottom right-hand tip of phyllo over the filling to meet the other side in a triangle, then continue folding in a triangle. Brush each triangle with butter to seal the edges. Repeat with the remaining phyllo dough and filling.
5. Place the triangles in the two air fryer baskets. Bake, 6 at a time, in two baskets for about 3 to 4 minutes, or until the filo is golden brown and crisp.
6. Serve hot.

Cheese Corn Fritters

Servings: 6
Cooking Time: 15 Minutes
Ingredients:

- 1 egg
- 164g corn
- 2 green onions, diced
- 45g flour
- 29g breadcrumbs
- 117g cheddar cheese, shredded
- ½ tsp onion powder
- ½ tsp garlic powder
- 15g sour cream
- Pepper
- Salt

Directions:

1. In a large bowl, add all ingredients and mix until well combined.
2. Insert a crisper plate in the Ninja Foodi air fryer baskets.
3. Make patties from the mixture and place them in both baskets.
4. Select zone 1, then select "air fry" mode and set the temperature to 370 degrees F for 12 minutes. Press "match" to match zone 2 settings to zone 1. Press "start/stop" to begin. Turn halfway through.

Healthy Spinach Balls

Servings: 4
Cooking Time: 15 Minutes
Ingredients:

- 1 egg
- 29g breadcrumbs
- ½ medium onion, chopped
- 225g spinach, blanched & chopped
- 1 carrot, peel & grated
- 1 tbsp cornflour
- 1 tbsp nutritional yeast
- 1 tsp garlic, minced
- ½ tsp garlic powder
- Pepper
- Salt

Directions:

1. Add spinach and remaining ingredients into the mixing bowl and mix until well combined.
2. Insert a crisper plate in the Ninja Foodi air fryer baskets.
3. Make small balls from the spinach mixture and place them in both baskets.
4. Select zone 1, then select "air fry" mode and set the temperature to 390 degrees F for 10 minutes. Press "match" to match zone 2 settings to zone 1. Press "start/stop" to begin.

Vegetables And Sides Recipes

Air Fryer Vegetables

Servings: 2
Cooking Time: 15 Minutes
Ingredients:

- 1 courgette, diced
- 2 capsicums, diced
- 1 head broccoli, diced
- 1 red onion, diced
- Marinade
- 1 teaspoon smoked paprika
- 1 teaspoon garlic granules
- 1 teaspoon Herb de Provence
- Salt and black pepper, to taste
- 1½ tablespoon olive oil
- 2 tablespoons lemon juice

Directions:

1. Toss the veggies with the rest of the marinade ingredients in a bowl.
2. Spread the veggies in the air fryer baskets.
3. Return the air fryer basket 1 to Zone 1, and basket 2 to Zone 2 of the Ninja Foodi 2-Basket Air Fryer.
4. Choose the "Air Fry" mode for Zone 1 at 400 degrees F and 15 minutes of cooking time.
5. Select the "MATCH COOK" option to copy the settings for Zone 2.
6. Initiate cooking by pressing the START/PAUSE BUTTON.
7. Toss the veggies once cooked half way through.
8. Serve warm.

Nutrition:

- (Per serving) Calories 166 | Fat 3.2g |Sodium 437mg | Carbs 28.8g | Fiber 1.8g | Sugar 2.7g | Protein 5.8g

Bbq Corn

Servings: 4
Cooking Time: 10 Minutes
Ingredients:

- 450g can baby corn, drained & rinsed
- 56g BBQ sauce
- ½ tsp Sriracha sauce

Directions:

1. In a bowl, toss the baby corn with sriracha sauce and BBQ sauce until well coated.
2. Insert a crisper plate in the Ninja Foodi air fryer baskets.
3. Add the baby corn to both baskets.
4. Select zone 1, then select "air fry" mode and set the temperature to 390 degrees F for 10 minutes. Press "match" to match zone 2 settings to zone 1. Press "start/stop" to begin. Stir halfway through.

Nutrition:

- (Per serving) Calories 46 | Fat 0.1g |Sodium 446mg | Carbs 10.2g | Fiber 2.8g | Sugar 5.9g | Protein 0.9g

Stuffed Sweet Potatoes

Servings: 4
Cooking Time: 55 Minutes
Ingredients:

- 2 medium sweet potatoes
- 1 teaspoon olive oil
- 1 cup cooked chopped spinach, drained
- 1 cup shredded cheddar cheese, divided
- 2 cooked bacon strips, crumbled
- 1 green onion, chopped
- ¼ cup fresh cranberries, coarsely chopped
- ⅓ cup chopped pecans, toasted
- 2 tablespoons butter
- ¼ teaspoon kosher salt
- ¼ teaspoon pepper

Directions:

1. Brush the sweet potatoes with the oil.
2. Place a crisper plate in both drawers. Add one sweet potato to each drawer. Place the drawers in the unit.
3. Select zone 1, then AIR FRY, then set the temperature to 360 degrees F/ 180 degrees C with a 40-minute timer. To match zone 2 settings to zone 1, choose MATCH. To begin, select START/STOP.
4. Remove the sweet potatoes from the drawers after the timer has finished. Cut them in half lengthwise. Scoop out the pulp, leaving a ¼-inch thick shell. 5. Put the pulp in a large bowl and stir in the spinach, ¾ cup of cheese, bacon, onion, pecans, cranberries, butter, salt, and pepper.
5. Spoon the mixture into the potato shells, mounding the mixture slightly.
6. Place a crisper plate in each drawer. Put one filled potato into each drawer and insert them into the unit.
7. Select zone 1, then AIR FRY, then set the temperature to 360 degrees F/ 180 degrees C with a 10-minute timer. To match zone 2 settings to zone 1, choose MATCH. To begin, select START/STOP.
8. Sprinkle with the remaining ¼ cup of cheese. Cook using the same settings until the cheese is melted .

Fried Asparagus

Servings: 4
Cooking Time: 6 Minutes
Ingredients:

- ¼ cup mayonnaise
- 4 teaspoons olive oil
- 1½ teaspoons grated lemon zest
- 1 garlic clove, minced
- ½ teaspoon pepper
- ¼ teaspoon seasoned salt
- 1-pound fresh asparagus, trimmed
- 2 tablespoons shredded parmesan cheese
- Lemon wedges (optional)

Directions:

1. In a large bowl, combine the first 6 ingredients.
2. Add the asparagus| toss to coat.
3. Put a crisper plate in both drawers. Put the asparagus in a single layer in each drawer. Top with the parmesan cheese. Place the drawers into the unit.
4. Select zone 1, then AIR FRY, then set the temperature to 375 degrees F/ 190 degrees C with a 6-minute timer. To match zone 2 settings to zone 1, choose MATCH. To begin, select START/STOP.
5. Remove the asparagus from the drawers after the timer has finished.

Curly Fries

Servings: 6
Cooking Time: 20 Minutes
Ingredients:

- 2 spiralized zucchinis
- 1 cup flour
- 2 tablespoons paprika
- 1 teaspoon cayenne pepper
- 1 teaspoon garlic powder
- 1 teaspoon black pepper
- 1 teaspoon salt
- 2 eggs
- Olive oil or cooking spray

Directions:

1. Mix flour with paprika, cayenne pepper, garlic powder, black pepper, and salt in a bowl.
2. Beat eggs in another bowl and dip the zucchini in the eggs.
3. Coat the zucchini with the flour mixture and divide it into two crisper plates. 4. Spray the zucchini with cooking oil.
4. Return the crisper plate to the Ninja Foodi Dual Zone Air Fryer.
5. Choose the Air Fry mode for Zone 1 and set the temperature to 400 degrees F/ 200 degrees C and the time to 20 minutes.
6. Select the "MATCH" button to copy the settings for Zone 2.
7. Initiate cooking by pressing the START/STOP button.
8. Toss the zucchini once cooked halfway through, then resume cooking.
9. Serve warm.

Herb And Lemon Cauliflower

Servings: 4
Cooking Time: 10 Minutes
Ingredients:

- 1 medium cauliflower, cut into florets (about 6 cups)
- 4 tablespoons olive oil, divided
- ¼ cup minced fresh parsley
- 1 tablespoon minced fresh rosemary
- 1 tablespoon minced fresh thyme
- 1 teaspoon grated lemon zest
- 2 tablespoons lemon juice
- ½ teaspoon salt
- ¼ teaspoon crushed red pepper flakes

Directions:

1. In a large bowl, combine the cauliflower florets and 2 tablespoons olive oil| toss to coat.
2. Put a crisper plate in both drawers, then put the cauliflower in a single layer in each. Insert the drawers into the unit.
3. Select zone 1, then AIR FRY, then set the temperature to 350 degrees F/ 175 degrees C with a 10-minute timer. To match zone 2 settings to zone 1, choose MATCH. To begin, select START/STOP.
4. Remove the cauliflower from the drawers after the timer has finished.
5. In a small bowl, combine the remaining ingredients. Stir in the remaining 2 tablespoons of oil.
6. Transfer the cauliflower to a large bowl and drizzle with the herb mixture. Toss to combine.

Air-fried Tofu Cutlets With Cacio E Pepe Brussels Sprouts

Servings:4
Cooking Time: 25 Minutes
Ingredients:

- FOR THE TOFU CUTLETS
- 1 (14-ounce) package extra-firm tofu, drained
- 1 cup panko bread crumbs
- ¼ cup grated pecorino romano or Parmesan cheese
- 1 teaspoon garlic powder
- 1 teaspoon onion powder
- ¼ teaspoon kosher salt
- 1 tablespoon vegetable oil
- 4 lemon wedges, for serving
- FOR THE BRUSSELS SPROUTS
- 1 pound Brussels sprouts, trimmed
- 1 tablespoon vegetable oil
- 2 tablespoons grated pecorino romano or Parmesan cheese
- ½ teaspoon freshly ground black pepper, plus more to taste
- ¼ teaspoon kosher salt

Directions:

1. To prep the tofu: Cut the tofu horizontally into 4 slabs.
2. In a shallow bowl, mix together the panko, cheese, garlic powder, onion powder, and salt. Press both sides of each tofu slab into the panko mixture. Drizzle both sides with the oil.
3. To prep the Brussels sprouts: Cut the Brussels sprouts in half through the root end.
4. In a large bowl, combine the Brussels sprouts and olive oil. Mix to coat.
5. To cook the tofu cutlets and Brussels sprouts: Install a crisper plate in each of the two baskets. Place the tofu cutlets in a single layer in the Zone 1 basket and insert the basket in the unit. Place the Brussels sprouts in the Zone 2 basket and insert the basket in the unit.
6. Select Zone 1, select AIR FRY, set the temperature to 400°F, and set the timer to 20 minutes.
7. Select Zone 2, select ROAST, set the temperature to 400°F, and set the timer to 25 minutes. Select SMART FINISH.
8. Press START/PAUSE to begin cooking.
9. When both timers read 5 minutes, press START/PAUSE. Remove the Zone 1 basket and use a pair of silicone-tipped tongs to flip the tofu cutlets, then reinsert the basket in the unit. Remove the Zone 2 basket and sprinkle the cheese and black pepper over the Brussels sprouts. Reinsert the basket and press START/PAUSE to resume cooking.
10. When cooking is complete, the tofu should be crisp and the Brussels sprouts tender and beginning to brown.
11. Squeeze the lemon wedges over the tofu cutlets. Stir the Brussels sprouts, then season with the salt and additional black pepper to taste.

Nutrition:

- (Per serving) Calories: 319; Total fat: 15g; Saturated fat: 3.5g; Carbohydrates: 27g; Fiber: 6g; Protein: 20g; Sodium: 402mg

Falafel

Servings: 6
Cooking Time: 14 Minutes
Ingredients:

- 1 (15.5-oz) can chickpeas, rinsed and drained
- 1 small yellow onion, cut into quarters
- 3 garlic cloves, chopped
- ⅓ cup parsley, chopped
- ⅓ cup cilantro, chopped
- ⅓ cup scallions, chopped
- 1 teaspoon cumin
- ½ teaspoons salt
- ⅛ teaspoons crushed red pepper flakes
- 1 teaspoon baking powder
- 4 tablespoons all-purpose flour
- Olive oil spray

Directions:

1. Dry the chickpeas on paper towels.
2. Add onions and garlic to a food processor and chop them.
3. Add the parsley, salt, cilantro, scallions, cumin, and red pepper flakes.
4. Press the pulse button for 60 seconds, then toss in chickpeas and blend for 3 times until it makes a chunky paste.
5. Stir in baking powder and flour and mix well.
6. Transfer the falafel mixture to a bowl and cover to refrigerate for 3 hours.
7. Make 12 balls out of the falafel mixture.
8. Place 6 falafels in each of the crisper plate and spray them with oil.
9. Return the crisper plate to the Ninja Foodi Dual Zone Air Fryer.
10. Choose the Air Fry mode for Zone 1 and set the temperature to 350 degrees F/ 175 degrees C and the time to 14 minutes.
11. Select the "MATCH" button to copy the settings for Zone 2.
12. Initiate cooking by pressing the START/STOP button.
13. Toss the falafel once cooked halfway through, and resume cooking.
14. Serve warm.

Hasselback Potatoes

Servings: 4
Cooking Time: 15 Minutes
Ingredients:

- 4 medium Yukon Gold potatoes
- 3 tablespoons melted butter
- 1 tablespoon olive oil
- 3 garlic cloves, crushed
- ½ teaspoon ground paprika
- Salt and black pepper ground, to taste
- 1 tablespoon chopped fresh parsley

Directions:

1. Slice each potato from the top to make ¼-inch slices without cutting its ½-inch bottom, keeping the potato's bottom intact.
2. Mix butter with olive oil, garlic, and paprika in a small bowl.
3. Brush the garlic mixture on top of each potato and add the mixture into the slits.
4. Season them with salt and black pepper.
5. Place 2 seasoned potatoes in each of the crisper plate.
6. Return the crisper plate to the Ninja Foodi Dual Zone Air Fryer.
7. Choose the Air Fry mode for Zone 1 and set the temperature to 375 degrees F/ 190 degrees C and the time to 25 minutes.
8. Select the "MATCH" button to copy the settings for Zone 2.
9. Initiate cooking by pressing the START/STOP button.
10. Brushing the potatoes again with butter mixture after 15 minutes, then resume cooking.
11. Garnish with parsley.
12. Serve warm.

Kale And Spinach Chips

Servings: 2
Cooking Time: 6 Minutes
Ingredients:

- 2 cups spinach, torn in pieces and stem removed
- 2 cups kale, torn in pieces, stems removed
- 1 tablespoon olive oil
- Sea salt, to taste
- ⅓ cup Parmesan cheese

Directions:

1. Take a bowl and add spinach to it.
2. Take another bowl and add kale to it.
3. Season both of them with olive oil and sea salt.
4. Add the kale to the zone 1 basket and spinach to the zone 2 basket.
5. Select AIR FRY mode for zone 1 at 350 degrees F/ 175 degrees C for 6 minutes.
6. Set zone 2 to AIR FRY mode at 350 degrees F/ 175 degrees C for 5 minutes.
7. Once done, take out the crispy chips and sprinkle Parmesan cheese on top. 8. Serve and Enjoy.

Air Fried Okra

Servings: 2

Cooking Time: 13 Minutes

Ingredients:

- ½ lb. okra pods sliced
- 1 teaspoon olive oil
- ¼ teaspoon salt
- ⅛ teaspoon black pepper

Directions:

1. Preheat the Ninja Foodi Dual Zone Air Fryer to 350 degrees F/ 175 degrees C.
2. Toss okra with olive oil, salt, and black pepper in a bowl.
3. Spread the okra in a single layer in the two crisper plates.
4. Return the crisper plate to the Ninja Foodi Dual Zone Air Fryer.
5. Choose the Air Fry mode for Zone 1 and set the temperature to 375 degrees F/ 190 degrees C and the time to 13 minutes.
6. Select the "MATCH" button to copy the settings for Zone 2.
7. Initiate cooking by pressing the START/STOP button.
8. Toss the okra once cooked halfway through, and resume cooking.
9. Serve warm.

Buffalo Bites

Servings: 6

Cooking Time: 30 Minutes

Ingredients:

- For the bites:
- 1 small cauliflower head, cut into florets
- 2 tablespoons olive oil
- 3 tablespoons buffalo wing sauce
- 3 tablespoons butter, melted
- For the dip:
- 1½ cups 2% cottage cheese
- ¼ cup fat-free plain Greek yogurt
- ¼ cup crumbled blue cheese
- 1 sachet ranch salad dressing mix
- Celery sticks (optional)

Directions:

1. In a large bowl, combine the cauliflower and oil| toss to coat.
2. Place a crisper plate in each drawer. Put the coated cauliflower florets in each drawer in a single layer. Place the drawers in the unit.
3. Select zone 1, then AIR FRY, then set the temperature to 360 degrees F/ 180 degrees C with a 15-minute timer. To match zone 2 settings to zone 1, choose MATCH. To begin, select START/STOP.
4. Remove the cauliflower from the drawers after the timer has finished.
5. Combine the buffalo sauce and melted butter in a large mixing bowl. Put in the cauliflower and toss to coat. Place on a serving dish and serve.
6. Combine the dip ingredients in a small bowl. Serve with the cauliflower and celery sticks, if desired.

Fried Olives

Servings: 6

Cooking Time: 9 Minutes

Ingredients:

- 2 cups blue cheese stuffed olives, drained
- ½ cup all-purpose flour
- 1 cup panko breadcrumbs
- ½ teaspoon garlic powder
- 1 pinch oregano
- 2 eggs

Directions:

1. Mix flour with oregano and garlic powder in a bowl and beat two eggs in another bowl.
2. Spread panko breadcrumbs in a bowl.
3. Coat all the olives with the flour mixture, dip in the eggs and then coat with the panko breadcrumbs.
4. As you coat the olives, place them in the two crisper plates in a single layer, then spray them with cooking oil.
5. Return the crisper plates to the Ninja Foodi Dual Zone Air Fryer.
6. Choose the Air Fry mode for Zone 1 and set the temperature to 375 degrees F/ 190 degrees C and the time to 9 minutes.
7. Select the "MATCH" button to copy the settings for Zone 2.
8. Initiate cooking by pressing the START/STOP button.
9. Flip the olives once cooked halfway through, then resume cooking.
10. Serve.

Spanakopita Rolls With Mediterranean Vegetable Salad

Servings:4
Cooking Time: 15 Minutes
Ingredients:

- FOR THE SPANAKOPITA ROLLS
- 1 (10-ounce) package chopped frozen spinach, thawed
- 4 ounces feta cheese, crumbled
- 2 large eggs
- 1 teaspoon dried oregano
- ½ teaspoon freshly ground black pepper
- 12 sheets phyllo dough, thawed
- Nonstick cooking spray
- FOR THE ROASTED VEGETABLES
- 1 medium eggplant, diced
- 1 small red onion, cut into 8 wedges
- 1 red bell pepper, sliced
- 2 tablespoons olive oil
- FOR THE SALAD
- 1 (15-ounce) can chickpeas, drained and rinsed
- ¼ cup chopped fresh parsley
- ¼ cup olive oil
- ¼ cup red wine vinegar
- 2 garlic cloves, minced
- ½ teaspoon dried oregano
- ¼ teaspoon kosher salt
- ¼ teaspoon freshly ground black pepper

Directions:

1. To prep the spanakopita rolls: Squeeze as much liquid from the spinach as you can and place the spinach in a large bowl. Add the feta, eggs, oregano, and black pepper. Mix well.
2. Lay one sheet of phyllo on a clean work surface and mist it with cooking spray. Place another sheet of phyllo directly on top of the first sheet and mist it with cooking spray. Repeat with a third sheet.
3. Spoon one-quarter of the spinach mixture along one short side of the phyllo. Fold the long sides in over the spinach, then roll up it like a burrito.
4. Repeat this process with the remaining phyllo sheets and spinach mixture to form 4 rolls.
5. To prep the vegetables: In a large bowl, combine the eggplant, onion, bell pepper, and oil. Mix well.
6. To cook the rolls and vegetables: Install a crisper plate in each of the two baskets. Place the spanakopita rolls seam-side down in the Zone 1 basket, and spritz the rolls with cooking spray. Place the vegetables in the Zone 2 basket and insert both baskets in the unit.
7. Select Zone 1, select AIR FRY, set the temperature to 375°F, and set the timer to 10 minutes.
8. Select Zone 2, select ROAST, set the temperature to 375°F, and set the timer to 15 minutes. Select SMART FINISH.
9. Press START/PAUSE to begin cooking.
10. When the Zone 1 timer reads 3 minutes, press START/PAUSE. Remove the basket and use silicone-tipped tongs or a spatula to flip the spanakopita rolls. Reinsert the basket and press START/PAUSE to resume cooking.
11. When cooking is complete, the rolls should be crisp and golden brown and the vegetables tender.
12. To assemble the salad: Transfer the roasted vegetables to a large bowl. Stir in the chickpeas and parsley.
13. In a small bowl, whisk together the oil, vinegar, garlic, oregano, salt, and black pepper. Pour the dressing over the vegetables and toss to coat. Serve warm.

Nutrition:

- (Per serving) Calories: 739; Total fat: 51g; Saturated fat: 8g; Carbohydrates: 67g; Fiber: 11g; Protein: 21g; Sodium: 806mg

Stuffed Tomatoes

Servings: 2
Cooking Time: 8 Minutes
Ingredients:

- 2 cups brown rice, cooked
- 1 cup tofu, grilled and chopped
- 4 large red tomatoes
- 4 tablespoons basil, chopped
- ¼ tablespoon olive oil
- Salt and black pepper, to taste
- 2 tablespoons lemon juice
- 1 teaspoon red chili powder
- ½ cup Parmesan cheese

Directions:

1. Take a large bowl and mix rice, tofu, basil, olive oil, salt, black pepper, lemon juice, and chili powder.
2. Core the center of the tomatoes.
3. Fill the cavity with the rice mixture.
4. Top them off with the cheese sprinkle.
5. Divide the tomatoes into two air fryer baskets.
6. Turn zone 1 to AIR FRY mode for 8 minutes at 400 degrees F/ 200 degrees C.
7. Select the MATCH button for zone 2.
8. Serve and enjoy.

Potato And Parsnip Latkes With Baked Apples

Servings:4

Cooking Time: 20 Minutes

Ingredients:

- FOR THE LATKES
- 2 medium russet potatoes, peeled
- 1 large egg white
- 2 tablespoons all-purpose flour
- ¼ teaspoon garlic powder
- ¼ teaspoon kosher salt
- ¼ teaspoon freshly ground black pepper
- 1 medium parsnip, peeled and shredded
- 2 scallions, thinly sliced
- 2 tablespoons vegetable oil
- FOR THE BAKED APPLES
- 2 Golden Delicious apples, peeled and diced
- 2 tablespoons granulated sugar
- 2 teaspoons unsalted butter, cut into small pieces

Directions:

1. To prep the latkes: Grate the potatoes using the large holes of a box grater. Squeeze as much liquid out of the potatoes as you can into a large bowl. Set the potatoes aside in a separate bowl.
2. Let the potato liquid sit for 5 minutes, during which time the potato starch will settle to the bottom of the bowl. Pour off the water that has risen to the top, leaving the potato starch in the bowl.
3. Add the egg white, flour, salt, and black pepper to the potato starch to form a thick paste. Add the potatoes, parsnip, and scallions and mix well. Divide the mixture into 4 patties. Brush both sides of each patty with the oil.
4. To prep the baked apples: Place the apples in the Zone 2 basket. Sprinkle the sugar and butter over the top.
5. To cook the latkes and apples: Install a crisper plate in the Zone 1 basket. Place the latkes in the basket in a single layer, then insert the basket in the unit. Insert the Zone 2 basket in the unit.
6. Select Zone 1, select AIR FRY, set the temperature to 375°F, and set the timer to 15 minutes.
7. Select Zone 2, select BAKE, set the temperature to 330°F, and set the timer to 20 minutes. Select SMART FINISH.
8. Press START/PAUSE to begin cooking.
9. When both timers read 5 minutes, press START/PAUSE. Remove the Zone 1 basket and use silicone-tipped tongs or a spatula to flip the latkes. Reinsert the basket in the unit. Remove the Zone 2 basket and gently mash the apples with a fork or the back of a spoon. Reinsert the basket and press START/PAUSE to resume cooking.
10. When cooking is complete, the latkes should be golden brown and cooked through and the apples very soft.
11. Transfer the latkes to a plate and serve with apples on the side.

Nutrition:

- (Per serving) Calories: 257; Total fat: 9g; Saturated fat: 2g; Carbohydrates: 42g; Fiber: 5.5g; Protein: 4g; Sodium: 91mg

Rosemary Asparagus & Potatoes

Servings: 6

Cooking Time: 30 Minutes

Ingredients:

- 125g asparagus, trimmed & cut into pieces
- 2 tsp garlic powder
- 2 tbsp rosemary, chopped
- 30ml olive oil
- 679g baby potatoes, quartered
- ½ tsp red pepper flakes
- Pepper
- Salt

Directions:

1. Insert a crisper plate in the Ninja Foodi air fryer baskets.
2. Toss potatoes with 1 tablespoon of oil, pepper, and salt in a bowl until well coated.
3. Add potatoes into in zone 1 basket.
4. Toss asparagus with remaining oil, red pepper flakes, pepper, garlic powder, and rosemary in a mixing bowl.
5. Add asparagus into the zone 2 basket.
6. Select zone 1, then select "air fry" mode and set the temperature to 390 degrees F for 20 minutes. Select zone 2, then select "air fry" mode and set the temperature to 390 degrees F for 10 minutes. Press "match" mode, then press "start/stop" to begin.

Nutrition:

- (Per serving) Calories 121 | Fat 5g |Sodium 40mg | Carbs 17.1g | Fiber 4.2g | Sugar 1g | Protein 4g

Veggie Burgers With "fried" Onion Rings

Servings:4

Cooking Time: 25 Minutes

Ingredients:

- FOR THE VEGGIE BURGERS
- 1 (15-ounce) can black beans, drained and rinsed
- ½ cup panko bread crumbs
- 1 large egg
- ¼ cup finely chopped red bell pepper
- ¼ cup frozen corn, thawed
- 1 tablespoon olive oil
- ½ teaspoon garlic powder
- ½ teaspoon ground cumin
- ¼ teaspoon smoked paprika
- Nonstick cooking spray
- 4 hamburger buns
- ¼ cup barbecue sauce, for serving
- FOR THE ONION RINGS
- 1 large sweet onion
- ½ cup all-purpose flour
- 2 large eggs
- 1 cup panko bread crumbs
- ½ teaspoon kosher salt
- Nonstick cooking spray

Directions:

1. To prep the veggie burgers: In a large bowl, mash the beans with a potato masher or a fork. Stir in the panko, egg, bell pepper, corn, oil, garlic powder, cumin, and smoked paprika. Mix well.
2. Shape the mixture into 4 patties. Spritz both sides of each patty with cooking spray.
3. To prep the onion rings: Cut the onion into ½-inch-thick rings.
4. Set up a breading station with three small shallow bowls. Place the flour in the first bowl. In the second bowl, beat the eggs. Place the panko and salt in the third bowl.
5. Bread the onions rings in this order: First, dip them into the flour, coating both sides. Then, dip into the beaten egg. Finally, coat them in the panko. Spritz each with cooking spray.
6. To cook the burgers and onion rings: Install a crisper plate in each of the two baskets. Place 2 veggie burgers in the Zone 1 basket. Place the onion rings in the Zone 2 basket and insert both baskets in the unit.
7. Select Zone 1, select AIR FRY, set the temperature to 390°F, and set the timer to 25 minutes.
8. Select Zone 2, select AIR FRY, set the temperature to 375°F, and set the timer to 10 minutes. Select SMART FINISH.
9. Press START/PAUSE to begin cooking.
10. When the Zone 1 timer reads 10 minutes, press START/PAUSE. Remove the basket and use a silicone spatula to flip the burgers. Reinsert the basket and press START/PAUSE to resume cooking.
11. When the Zone 1 timer reads 10 minutes, press START/PAUSE. Remove the basket and transfer the burgers to a plate. Place the 2 remaining burgers in the basket. Reinsert the basket and press START/PAUSE to resume cooking.
12. When both timers read 5 minutes, press START/PAUSE. Remove the Zone 1 basket and flip the burgers, then reinsert the basket. Remove the Zone 2 basket and shake vigorously to rearrange the onion rings and separate any that have stuck together. Reinsert the basket and press START/PAUSE to resume cooking.
13. When cooking is complete, the veggie burgers should be cooked through and the onion rings golden brown.
14. Place 1 burger on each bun. Top with barbecue sauce and serve with onion rings on the side.

Nutrition:

- (Per serving) Calories: 538; Total fat: 16g; Saturated fat: 2g; Carbohydrates: 83g; Fiber: 10g; Protein: 19g; Sodium: 914mg

Zucchini Cakes

Servings: 6

Cooking Time: 32 Minutes

Ingredients:

- 2 medium zucchinis, grated
- 1 cup corn kernel
- 1 medium potato cooked
- 2 tablespoons chickpea flour
- 2 garlic minced
- 2 teaspoons olive oil
- Salt and black pepper
- For Serving:
- Yogurt tahini sauce

Directions:

1. Mix grated zucchini with a pinch of salt in a colander and leave them for 15 minutes.
2. Squeeze out their excess water.
3. Mash the cooked potato in a large-sized bowl with a fork.

4. Add zucchini, corn, garlic, chickpea flour, salt, and black pepper to the bowl. 5. Mix these fritters' ingredients together and make 2 tablespoons-sized balls out of this mixture and flatten them lightly.
5. Divide the fritters in the two crisper plates in a single layer and spray them with cooking.
6. Return the crisper plates to the Ninja Foodi Dual Zone Air Fryer.
7. Choose the Air Fry mode for Zone 1 and set the temperature to 390 degrees F/ 200 degrees C and the time to 17 minutes.
8. Select the "MATCH" button to copy the settings for Zone 2.
9. Initiate cooking by pressing the START/STOP button.
10. Flip the fritters once cooked halfway through, then resume cooking.
11. Serve.

Pepper Poppers

Servings: 24
Cooking Time: 20 Minutes
Ingredients:

- 8 ounces cream cheese, softened
- ¾ cup shredded cheddar cheese
- ¾ cup shredded Monterey Jack cheese
- 6 bacon strips, cooked and crumbled
- ¼ teaspoon salt
- ¼ teaspoon garlic powder
- ¼ teaspoon chili powder
- ¼ teaspoon smoked paprika
- 1-pound fresh jalapeño peppers, halved lengthwise and deseeded
- ½ cup dry breadcrumbs
- Sour cream, French onion dip, or ranch salad dressing (optional)

Directions:

1. In a large bowl, combine the cheeses, bacon, and seasonings| mix well. Spoon 1½ to 2 tablespoons of the mixture into each pepper half. Roll them in the breadcrumbs.
2. Place a crisper plate in each drawer. Put the prepared peppers in a single layer in each drawer. Insert the drawers into the unit.
3. Select zone 1, then AIR FRY, then set the temperature to 360 degrees F/ 180 degrees C with a 20-minute timer. To match zone 2 settings to zone 1, choose MATCH. To begin, select START/STOP.
4. Remove the peppers from the drawers after the timer has finished.

Sweet Potatoes With Honey Butter

Servings: 4
Cooking Time: 40 Minutes
Ingredients:

- 4 sweet potatoes, scrubbed
- 1 teaspoon oil
- Honey Butter
- 4 tablespoons unsalted butter
- 1 tablespoon Honey
- 2 teaspoons hot sauce
- ¼ teaspoon salt

Directions:

1. Rub the sweet potatoes with oil and place two potatoes in each crisper plate. 2. Return the crisper plate to the Ninja Foodi Dual Zone Air Fryer.
2. Choose the Air Fry mode for Zone 1 and set the temperature to 400 degrees F/ 200 degrees C and the time to 40 minutes.
3. Select the "MATCH" button to copy the settings for Zone 2.
4. Initiate cooking by pressing the START/STOP button.
5. Flip the potatoes once cooked halfway through, then resume cooking.
6. Mix butter with hot sauce, honey, and salt in a bowl.
7. When the potatoes are done, cut a slit on top and make a well with a spoon 9. Pour the honey butter in each potato jacket.
8. Serve.

Beef, Pork, And Lamb Recipes

Marinated Steak & Mushrooms

Servings: 4
Cooking Time: 10 Minutes

Ingredients:

- 450g rib-eye steak, cut into ½-inch pieces
- 2 tsp dark soy sauce
- 2 tsp light soy sauce
- 15ml lime juice
- 15ml rice wine
- 15ml oyster sauce
- 1 tbsp garlic, chopped
- 8 mushrooms, sliced
- 2 tbsp ginger, grated
- 1 tsp cornstarch
- ¼ tsp pepper

Directions:

1. Add steak pieces, mushrooms, and the remaining ingredients to a zip-lock bag. Seal the bag and place it in the refrigerator for 2 hours.
2. Insert a crisper plate in the Ninja Foodi air fryer baskets.
3. Remove the steak pieces and mushrooms from the marinade and place them in both baskets.
4. Select zone 1, then select "air fry" mode and set the temperature to 380 degrees F for 10 minutes. Press "match" to match zone 2 settings to zone 1. Press "start/stop" to begin. Stir halfway through.

Garlic Butter Steak Bites

Servings: 3
Cooking Time: 16 Minutes

Ingredients:

- Oil, for spraying
- 450 g boneless steak, cut into 1-inch pieces
- 2 tablespoons olive oil
- 1 teaspoon Worcestershire sauce
- ½ teaspoon granulated garlic
- ½ teaspoon salt
- ¼ teaspoon freshly ground black pepper

Directions:

1. Preheat the air fryer to 204°C. Line the two air fryer drawers with parchment and spray lightly with oil.
2. In a medium bowl, combine the steak, olive oil, Worcestershire sauce, garlic, salt, and black pepper and toss until evenly coated.
3. Place the steak in a single layer in the two prepared drawers.
4. Cook for 10 to 16 minutes, flipping every 3 to 4 minutes. The total cooking time will depend on the thickness of the meat and your preferred doneness. If you want it well done, it may take up to 5 additional minutes.

Breaded Pork Chops

Servings: 4
Cooking Time: 10 Minutes

Ingredients:

- 4 boneless, center-cut pork chops, 1-inch thick
- 1 teaspoon Cajun seasoning
- 1½ cups cheese and garlic-flavored croutons
- 2 eggs
- Cooking spray

Directions:

1. Season both sides of the pork chops with the Cajun seasoning on a platter.
2. In a small food processor, pulse the croutons until finely chopped; transfer to a shallow plate.
3. In a separate shallow bowl, lightly beat the eggs.
4. Dip the pork chops in the egg, allowing any excess to drip off. Then place the chops in the crouton crumbs. Coat the chops in cooking spray.
5. Install a crisper plate in both drawers. Place half the pork chops in the zone 1 drawer and half in zone 2's, then insert the drawers into the unit.
6. Select zone 1, select ROAST, set temperature to 390 degrees F/ 200 degrees C, and set time to 10 minutes. Select MATCH to match zone 2 settings to zone 1. Press the START/STOP button to begin cooking.
7. When the time reaches 6 minutes, press START/STOP to pause the unit. Remove the drawers and flip the chops. Reinsert the drawers into the unit and press START/STOP to resume cooking.
8. When cooking is complete, serve and enjoy!

Nutrition:

- (Per serving) Calories 394 | Fat 18.1g | Sodium 428mg | Carbs 10g | Fiber 0.8g | Sugar 0.9g | Protein 44.7g

Asian Pork Skewers

Servings: 4

Cooking Time: 30 Minutes

Ingredients:

- 450g pork shoulder, sliced
- 30g ginger, peeled and crushed
- ½ tablespoon crushed garlic
- 67½ml soy sauce
- 22½ml honey
- 22½ml rice vinegar
- 10ml toasted sesame oil
- 8 skewers

Directions:

1. Pound the pork slices with a mallet.
2. Mix ginger, garlic, soy sauce, honey, rice vinegar, and sesame oil in a bowl.
3. Add pork slices to the marinade and mix well to coat.
4. Cover and marinate the pork for 30 minutes.
5. Thread the pork on the wooden skewers and place them in the air fryer baskets.
6. Return the air fryer basket 1 to Zone 1, and basket 2 to Zone 2 of the Ninja Foodi 2-Basket Air Fryer.
7. Choose the "Air Fry" mode for Zone 1 and set the temperature to 350 degrees F and 25 minutes of cooking time.
8. Select the "MATCH COOK" option to copy the settings for Zone 2.
9. Initiate cooking by pressing the START/PAUSE BUTTON.
10. Flip the skewers once cooked halfway through.
11. Serve warm.

Steak In Air Fry

Servings:1

Cooking Time:20

Ingredients:

- 2 teaspoons of canola oil
- 1 tablespoon of Montreal steaks seasoning
- 1 pound of beef steak

Directions:

1. The first step is to season the steak on both sides with canola oil and then rub a generous amount of steak seasoning all over.
2. We are using the AIR BROIL feature of the ninja air fryer and it works with one basket.
3. Put the steak in the basket and set it to AIR BROIL at 450 degrees F for 20 -22 minutes.
4. After 7 minutes, hit pause and take out the basket to flip the steak, and cover it with foil on top, for the remaining 14 minutes.
5. Once done, serve the medium-rare steak and enjoy it by resting for 10 minutes.
6. Serve by cutting in slices.
7. Enjoy.

Nutrition:

- (Per serving) Calories 935| Fat 37.2g| Sodium 1419mg | Carbs 0g | Fiber 0g| Sugar 0g | Protein137.5 g

Steak And Mashed Creamy Potatoes

Servings:1

Cooking Time:45

Ingredients:

- 2 Russet potatoes, peeled and cubed
- ¼ cup butter, divided
- 1/3 cup heavy cream
- ½ cup shredded cheddar cheese
- Salt and black pepper, to taste
- 1 New York strip steak, about a pound
- 1 teaspoon of olive oil
- Oil spray, for greasing

Directions:

1. Rub the potatoes with salt and a little amount of olive oil about a teaspoon.
2. Next, season the steak with salt and black pepper.
3. Place the russet potatoes in a zone 1 basket.
4. Oil spray the steak from both sides and then place it in the zone 2 basket.
5. Set zone 1 to AIR fry mode for 45 minutes at 390 degrees F.
6. Set the zone 2 basket, at 12 minutes at 375 degrees F.
7. Hot start and Lethe ninja foodie do its magic.
8. One the cooking cycle completes, take out the steak and potatoes.
9. Mash the potatoes and then add butter, heavy cream, and cheese along with salt and black pepper.
10. Serve the mashed potatoes with steak.
11. Enjoy.

Nutrition:

- (Per serving) Calories1932 | Fat 85.2g| Sodium 3069mg | Carbs 82g | Fiber10.3 g| Sugar 5.3g | Protein 22.5g

Tender Pork Chops

Servings: 2

Cooking Time: 20 Minutes

Ingredients:

- 2 pork chops
- 1 tsp dry mustard
- 1 tsp ground coriander
- 1 tbsp chilli powder
- 30ml olive oil
- ¼ tsp cayenne
- ½ tsp ground cumin
- 1 tsp smoked paprika
- Pepper
- Salt

Directions:

1. In a small bowl, mix chilli powder, paprika, cayenne, coriander, mustard, pepper, and salt.
2. Brush the pork chops with oil and rub with spice mixture.
3. Insert a crisper plate in the Ninja Foodi air fryer baskets.
4. Place the chops in both baskets.
5. Select zone 1, then select "air fry" mode and set the temperature to 375 degrees F for 10 minutes. Press "match" to match zone 2 settings to zone 1. Press "start/stop" to begin. Turn halfway through.

Pork With Green Beans And Potatoes

Servings: 4

Cooking Time: 15 Minutes.

Ingredients:

- ¼ cup Dijon mustard
- 2 tablespoons brown sugar
- 1 teaspoon dried parsley flake
- ½ teaspoon dried thyme
- ¼ teaspoons salt
- ¼ teaspoons black pepper
- 1 ¼ lbs. pork tenderloin
- ¾ lb. small potatoes halved
- 1 (12-oz) package green beans, trimmed
- 1 tablespoon olive oil
- Salt and black pepper ground to taste

Directions:

1. Preheat your Air Fryer Machine to 400 degrees F.
2. Add mustard, parsley, brown sugar, salt, black pepper, and thyme in a large bowl, then mix well.
3. Add tenderloin to the spice mixture and coat well.
4. Toss potatoes with olive oil, salt, black pepper, and green beans in another bowl.
5. Place the prepared tenderloin in the crisper plate.
6. Return this crisper plate to the Zone 1 of the Ninja Foodi Dual Zone Air Fryer.
7. Choose the Air Fry mode for Zone 1 and set the temperature to 390 degrees F and the time to 15 minutes.
8. Add potatoes and green beans to the Zone 2.
9. Choose the Air Fry mode for Zone 2 with 350 degrees F and the time to 10 minutes.
10. Press the SYNC button to sync the finish time for both Zones.
11. Initiate cooking by pressing the START/STOP button.
12. Serve the tenderloin with Air Fried potatoes

Nutrition:

- (Per serving) Calories 400 | Fat 32g |Sodium 721mg | Carbs 2.6g | Fiber 0g | Sugar 0g | Protein 27.4g

Garlic Sirloin Steak

Servings: 4

Cooking Time: 10 Minutes

Ingredients:

- 4 sirloin steak
- 30ml olive oil
- 28g steak sauce
- ½ tsp ground coriander
- 1 tsp garlic, minced
- 1 tbsp thyme, chopped
- Pepper
- Salt

Directions:

1. In a bowl, mix steak with thyme, oil, steak sauce, coriander, garlic, pepper, and salt. Cover and set aside for 2 hours.
2. Insert a crisper plate in Ninja Foodi air fryer baskets.
3. Place the marinated steaks in both baskets.
4. Select zone 1 then select air fry mode and set the temperature to 360 degrees F for 10 minutes. Press "match" and then "start/stop" to begin.

Bbq Pork Loin

Servings: 6

Cooking Time: 30 Minutes

Ingredients:

- 1 (1-pound) pork loin
- 2-3 tablespoons barbecue seasoning rub
- 2 tablespoons olive oil

Directions:

1. Coat each pork loin with oil and then rub with barbecue seasoning rub generously.
2. Grease each basket of "Zone 1" and "Zone 2" of Ninja Foodi 2-Basket Air Fryer.
3. Press "Zone 1" and "Zone 2" and then rotate the knob for each zone to select "Bake".
4. Set the temperature to 350 degrees F/ 175 degrees C for both zones and then set the time for 5 minutes to preheat.
5. After preheating, arrange pork loin into the basket of each zone.
6. Slide each basket into Air Fryer and set the time for 30 minutes.
7. After cooking time is completed, remove each pork loin from Air Fryer and place onto a platter for about 10 minutes before slicing.
8. With a sharp knife, cut each pork loin into desired-sized slices and serve.

Italian Sausages With Peppers And Teriyaki Rump Steak With Broccoli

Servings: 7

Cooking Time: 28 Minutes

Ingredients:

- Italian Sausages with Peppers:
- 1 medium onion, thinly sliced
- 1 yellow or orange pepper, thinly sliced
- 1 red pepper, thinly sliced
- 60 ml avocado oil or melted coconut oil
- 1 teaspoon fine sea salt
- 6 Italian-seasoned sausages
- Dijon mustard, for serving (optional)
- Teriyaki Rump Steak with Broccoli:
- 230 g rump steak
- 80 ml teriyaki marinade
- 1½ teaspoons sesame oil
- ½ head broccoli, cut into florets
- 2 red peppers, sliced
- Fine sea salt and ground black pepper, to taste
- Cooking spray

Directions:

1. Make the Italian Sausages with Peppers :
2. Preheat the air fryer to 204°C.
3. Place the onion and peppers in a large bowl. Drizzle with the oil and toss well to coat the veggies. Season with the salt.
4. Place the onion and peppers in a pie pan and cook in the air fryer for 8 minutes, stirring halfway through. Remove from the air fryer and set aside.
5. Spray the zone 1 air fryer drawer with avocado oil. Place the sausages in the zone 1 air fryer drawer and air fry for 20 minutes, or until crispy and golden brown. During the last minute or two of cooking, add the onion and peppers to the drawer with the sausages to warm them through.
6. Place the onion and peppers on a serving platter and arrange the sausages on top. Serve Dijon mustard on the side, if desired.
7. Store leftovers in an airtight container in the fridge for up to 7 days or in the freezer for up to a month. Reheat in a preheated 200°C air fryer for 3 minutes, or until heated through.
8. Make the Teriyaki Rump Steak with Broccoli :
9. Toss the rump steak in a large bowl with teriyaki marinade. Wrap the bowl in plastic and refrigerate to marinate for at least an hour.
10. Preheat the air fryer to 204°C and spritz with cooking spray.
11. Discard the marinade and transfer the steak in the preheated zone 2 air fryer drawer. Spritz with cooking spray.
12. Air fry for 13 minutes or until well browned. Flip the steak halfway through.
13. Meanwhile, heat the sesame oil in a nonstick skillet over medium heat. Add the broccoli and red pepper. Sprinkle with salt and ground black pepper. Sauté for 5 minutes or until the broccoli is tender.
14. Transfer the air fried rump steak on a plate and top with the sautéed broccoli and pepper. Serve hot.

Beef Ribs Ii

Servings:2

Cooking Time:1

Ingredients:

- ¼ cup olive oil
- 4 garlic cloves, minced
- ½ cup white wine vinegar
- ¼ cup soy sauce, reduced-sodium
- ¼ cup Worcestershire sauce
- 1 lemon juice
- Salt and black pepper, to taste
- 2 tablespoons of Italian seasoning
- 1 teaspoon of smoked paprika
- 2 tablespoons of mustard
- ½ cup maple syrup
- Meat Ingredients:
- Oil spray, for greasing
- 8 beef ribs lean

Directions:

1. Take a large bowl and add all the ingredients under marinade ingredients.
2. Put the marinade in a zip lock bag and add ribs to it.
3. Let it sit for 4 hours.
4. Now take out the basket of air fryer and grease the baskets with oil spray.
5. Now dived the ribs among two baskets.
6. Set it to AIR fry mode at 220 degrees F for 30 minutes.
7. Select Pause and take out the baskets.
8. Afterward, flip the ribs and cook for 30 minutes at 250 degrees F.
9. Once done, serve the juicy and tender ribs.
10. Enjoy.

Nutrition:

- (Per serving) Calories 1927| Fat116g| Sodium 1394mg | Carbs 35.2g | Fiber 1.3g| Sugar29 g | Protein 172.3g

Honey Glazed Bbq Pork Ribs

Servings: 4

Cooking Time: 30 Minutes

Ingredients:

- 2 pounds pork ribs
- ¼ cup honey, divided
- 1 cup BBQ sauce
- ½ teaspoon garlic powder
- 2 tablespoons tomato ketchup
- 1 tablespoon Worcestershire sauce
- 1 tablespoon low-sodium soy sauce
- Freshly ground white pepper, as required

Directions:

1. In a bowl, mix together honey and the remaining ingredients except pork ribs.
2. Add the pork ribs and coat with the mixture generously.
3. Refrigerate to marinate for about 20 minutes.
4. Grease each basket of "Zone 1" and "Zone 2" of Ninja Foodi 2-Basket Air Fryer.
5. Press "Zone 1" and "Zone 2" and then rotate the knob for each zone to select "Air Fry".
6. Set the temperature to 355 degrees F/ 180 degrees C for both zones and then set the time for 5 minutes to preheat.
7. After preheating, arrange the ribs into the basket of each zone.
8. Slide each basket into Air Fryer and set the time for 26 minutes.
9. While cooking, flip the ribs once halfway through.
10. After cooking time is completed, remove the ribs from Air Fryer and place onto serving plates.
11. Drizzle with the remaining honey and serve immediately.

Simple Beef Sirloin Roast

Servings: 16

Cooking Time: 50 Minutes

Ingredients:

- 2 (2½-pound) sirloin roast
- Salt and ground black pepper, as required

Directions:

1. Grease each basket of "Zone 1" and "Zone 2" of Ninja Foodi 2-Basket Air Fryer.
2. Press "Zone 1" and "Zone 2" and then rotate the knob for each zone to select "Roast".
3. Set the temperature to 350 degrees F/ 175 degrees C for both zones and then set the time for 5 minutes to preheat.
4. Rub ach roast with salt and black pepper generously.
5. After preheating, arrange 1 roast into the basket of each zone.
6. Slide each basket into Air Fryer and set the time for 50 minutes.
7. After cooking time is completed, remove each roast from Air Fryer and place onto a platter for about 10 minutes before slicing.
8. With a sharp knife, cut each roast into desired-sized slices and serve.

Curry-crusted Lamb Chops With Baked Brown Sugar Acorn Squash

Servings:4
Cooking Time: 20 Minutes
Ingredients:

- FOR THE LAMB CHOPS
- 4 lamb loin chops (4 ounces each)
- 1 tablespoon olive oil
- 2 teaspoons curry powder
- ¼ teaspoon kosher salt
- FOR THE ACORN SQUASH
- 2 small acorn squash
- 4 teaspoons dark brown sugar
- 2 teaspoons salted butter
- ⅛ teaspoon kosher salt

Directions:

1. To prep the lamb chops: Brush both sides of the lamb chops with the oil and season with the curry powder and salt.
2. To prep the acorn squash: Cut the squash in half through the stem end and remove the seeds. Place 1 teaspoon of brown sugar and ½ teaspoon of butter into the well of each squash half.
3. To cook the lamb and squash: Install a crisper plate in each of the two baskets. Place the lamb chops in the Zone 1 basket and insert the basket in the unit. Place the squash cut-side up in the Zone 2 basket and insert the basket in the unit.
4. Select Zone 1, select AIR FRY, set the temperature to 400°F, and set the timer to 15 minutes.
5. Select Zone 2, select BAKE, set the temperature to 400°F, and set the time to 20 minutes. Select SMART FINISH.
6. Press START/PAUSE to begin cooking.
7. When both timers read 5 minutes, press START/PAUSE. Remove the Zone 1 basket and use a pair of silicone-tipped tongs to flip the lamb chops. Reinsert the basket in the unit. Remove the Zone 2 basket and spoon the melted butter and sugar over the top edges of the squash. Reinsert the basket and press START/PAUSE to resume cooking.
8. When cooking is complete, the lamb should be cooked to your liking and the squash soft when pierced with a fork.
9. Remove the lamb chops from the basket and let rest for 5 minutes. Season the acorn squash with salt before serving.

Nutrition:

- (Per serving) Calories: 328; Total fat: 19g; Saturated fat: 7.5g; Carbohydrates: 23g; Fiber: 3g; Protein: 16g; Sodium: 172mg

Cheesy Low-carb Lasagna

Servings: 4
Cooking Time: 10 Minutes
Ingredients:

- Meat Layer:
- Extra-virgin olive oil
- 450 g 85% lean beef mince
- 235 ml marinara sauce
- 60 ml diced celery
- 60 ml diced red onion
- ½ teaspoon minced garlic
- Coarse or flaky salt and black pepper, to taste
- Cheese Layer:
- 230 g ricotta cheese
- 235 ml shredded Mozzarella cheese
- 120 ml grated Parmesan cheese
- 2 large eggs
- 1 teaspoon dried Italian seasoning, crushed
- ½ teaspoon each minced garlic, garlic powder, and black pepper

Directions:

1. For the meat layer: Grease a cake pan with 1 teaspoon olive oil. 2. In a large bowl, combine the beef mince, marinara, celery, onion, garlic, salt, and pepper. Place the seasoned meat in the pan. 3. Place the pan in the zone 1 air fryer drawer. Set the temperature to 192°C for 10 minutes. 4. Meanwhile, for the cheese layer: In a medium bowl, combine the ricotta, half the Mozzarella, the Parmesan, lightly beaten eggs, Italian seasoning, minced garlic, garlic powder, and pepper. Stir until well blended. 5. At the end of the cooking time, spread the cheese mixture over the meat mixture. Sprinkle with the remaining 120 ml Mozzarella. Set the temperature to 192°C for 10 minutes, or until the cheese is browned and bubbling. 6. At the end of the cooking time, use a meat thermometer to ensure the meat has reached an internal temperature of 72°C. 7. Drain the fat and liquid from the pan. Let stand for 5 minutes before serving.

Simple Lamb Meatballs

Servings: 4
Cooking Time: 15 Minutes
Ingredients:

- 1-pound ground lamb
- 1 teaspoon ground cinnamon
- 1 teaspoon ground cumin
- 2 teaspoons granulated onion
- 2 tablespoons fresh parsley
- Salt and black pepper, to taste

Directions:

1. Add ground lamb, onion, cinnamon, cumin, parsley, salt and pepper in a large bowl. Mix until well combined.
2. Make 1-inch balls from the mixture and set aside.
3. Grease each basket of "Zone 1" and "Zone 2" of Ninja Foodi 2-Basket Air Fryer.
4. Press "Zone 1" and "Zone 2" and then rotate the knob for each zone to select "Air Fry".
5. Set the temperature to 380 degrees F/ 195 degrees C for both zones and then set the time for 5 minutes to preheat.
6. After preheating, arrange the meatballs into the basket of each zone.
7. Slide each basket into Air Fryer and set the time for 12 minutes.
8. Flip the meatballs once halfway through.
9. Take out and serve warm.

Roasted Beef

Servings: 8
Cooking Time: 50 Minutes
Ingredients:

- 1 (1-pound) beef roast
- Salt and ground black pepper, as required

Directions:

1. Grease each basket of "Zone 1" and "Zone 2" of Ninja Foodi 2-Basket Air Fryer.
2. Press "Zone 1" and "Zone 2" and then rotate the knob for each zone to select "Roast".
3. Set the temperature to 350 degrees F/ 175 degrees C for both zones and then set the time for 5 minutes to preheat.
4. Rub ach roast with salt and black pepper generously.
5. After preheating, arrange the roast into the basket of each zone.
6. Slide each basket into Air Fryer and set the time for 50 minutes.
7. After cooking time is completed, remove each roast from Air Fryer and place onto a platter for about 10 minutes before slicing.
8. With a sharp knife, cut each roast into desired-sized slices and serve.

Hot Dogs Wrapped In Bacon

Servings: 2
Cooking Time: 20 Minutes
Ingredients:

- 2 bacon strips
- 2 hot dogs
- Salt and black pepper, to taste

Directions:

1. Wrap each hot dog with bacon strip and season with salt and black pepper.
2. Grease each basket of "Zone 1" and "Zone 2" of Ninja Foodi 2-Basket Air Fryer.
3. Press "Zone 1" and "Zone 2" and then rotate the knob for each zone to select "Air Fry".
4. Set the temperature to 400 degrees F/ 200 degrees C for both zones and then set the time for 5 minutes to preheat.
5. After preheating, arrange bacon wrapped hot dogs into the basket of each zone.
6. Slide each basket into Air Fryer and set the time for 15 minutes.
7. While cooking, flip the hot dogs once halfway through.
8. After cooking time is completed, remove the filets from Air Fryer and serve hot.

Meatballs

Servings: 4
Cooking Time: 20 Minutes
Ingredients:

- 450g ground beef
- 59ml milk
- 45g parmesan cheese, grated
- 50g breadcrumbs
- ½ tsp Italian seasoning
- 2 garlic cloves, minced
- Pepper
- Salt

Directions:

1. In a bowl, mix the meat and remaining ingredients until well combined.
2. Insert a crisper plate in the Ninja Foodi air fryer baskets.
3. Make small balls from the meat mixture and place them in both baskets.
4. Select zone 1, then select "air fry" mode and set the temperature to 375 degrees F for 15 minutes. Press "match" and "start/stop" to begin.

Cinnamon-beef Kofta

Servings: 12 Koftas
Cooking Time: 13 Minutes

Ingredients:

- 680 g lean beef mince
- 1 teaspoon onion granules
- ¾ teaspoon ground cinnamon
- ¾ teaspoon ground dried turmeric
- 1 teaspoon ground cumin
- ¾ teaspoon salt
- ¼ teaspoon cayenne
- 12 (3½- to 4-inch-long) cinnamon sticks
- Cooking spray

Directions:

1. Preheat the air fryer to 192°C. Spritz the two air fryer drawers with cooking spray.
2. Combine all the ingredients, except for the cinnamon sticks, in a large bowl. Toss to mix well.
3. Divide and shape the mixture into 12 balls, then wrap each ball around each cinnamon stick and leave a quarter of the length uncovered.
4. Arrange the beef-cinnamon sticks in the preheated air fryer and spritz with cooking spray.
5. Air fry for 13 minutes or until the beef is browned. Flip the sticks halfway through.
6. Serve immediately.

Goat Cheese-stuffed Bavette Steak

Servings: 6
Cooking Time: 14 Minutes

Ingredients:

- 450 g bavette or skirt steak
- 1 tablespoon avocado oil
- ½ teaspoon sea salt
- ½ teaspoon garlic powder
- ¼ teaspoon freshly ground black pepper
- 60 g goat cheese, crumbled
- 235 ml baby spinach, chopped

Directions:

1. Place the steak in a large zip-top bag or between two pieces of plastic wrap. Using a meat mallet or heavy-bottomed skillet, pound the steak to an even ¼-inch thickness.
2. Brush both sides of the steak with the avocado oil.
3. Mix the salt, garlic powder, and pepper in a small dish. Sprinkle this mixture over both sides of the steak.
4. Sprinkle the goat cheese over top, and top that with the spinach.
5. Starting at one of the long sides, roll the steak up tightly. Tie the rolled steak with kitchen string at 3-inch intervals.
6. Set the zone 1 air fryer drawer to 204°C. Place the steak roll-up in the zone 1 air fryer drawer. Air fry for 7 minutes. Flip the steak and cook for an additional 7 minutes, until an instant-read thermometer reads 49°C for medium-rare .

Beef & Broccoli

Servings:4
Cooking Time:12

Ingredients:

- 12 ounces of teriyaki sauce, divided
- ½ tablespoon garlic powder
- ¼ cup of soy sauce
- 1 pound raw sirloin steak, thinly sliced
- 2 cups broccoli, cut into florets
- 2 teaspoons of olive oil
- Salt and black pepper, to taste

Directions:

1. Take a zip-lock plastic bag and mix teriyaki sauce, salt, garlic powder, black pepper, soy sauce, and olive oil.
2. Marinate the beef in it for 2 hours.
3. Then drain the beef from the marinade.
4. Now toss the broccoli with oil, teriyaki sauce, and salt and black pepper.
5. Put it in a zone 1 basket
6. Now for the zone, 1 basket set it to AIRFRY mode at 400 degrees F for 15 minutes.
7. Place the steak in a zone 2 basket and set it to AIR FRY mode at 375 degrees F for 10-12 minutes.
8. Hit start and let the cooking cycle completes.
9. Once it's done take out the beef and broccoli and
10. serve immediately with leftover teriyaki sauce and cooked rice.

Nutrition:

- (Per serving) Calories 344| Fat 10g| Sodium 4285mg | Carbs18.2 g | Fiber 1.5g| Sugar 13.3g | Protein42 g

Cinnamon-apple Pork Chops

Servings: 4
Cooking Time: 10 Minutes

Ingredients:

- 2 tablespoons butter
- 4 boneless pork loin chops
- 3 tablespoons brown sugar
- 1 teaspoon ground cinnamon
- ½ teaspoon ground nutmeg
- ¼ teaspoon salt
- 4 medium tart apples, sliced
- 2 tablespoons chopped pecans

Directions:

1. Mix butter, brown sugar, cinnamon, nutmeg, and salt in a bowl.
2. Rub this mixture over the pork chops and place them in the air fryer baskets.
3. Top them with apples and pecans.
4. Return the air fryer basket 1 to Zone 1, and basket 2 to Zone 2 of the Ninja Foodi 2-Basket Air Fryer.
5. Choose the "Air Fry" mode for Zone 1 at 375 degrees F and 10 minutes of cooking time.
6. Select the "MATCH COOK" option to copy the settings for Zone 2.
7. Initiate cooking by pressing the START/PAUSE BUTTON.
8. Serve warm.

Taco Seasoned Steak

Servings: 6
Cooking Time: 30 Minutes

Ingredients:

- 1 (1-pound) flank steaks
- 1½ tablespoons taco seasoning rub

Directions:

1. Grease each basket of "Zone 1" and "Zone 2" of Ninja Foodi 2-Basket Air Fryer.
2. Press "Zone 1" and "Zone 2" and then rotate the knob for each zone to select "Bake".
3. Set the temperature to 420 degrees F/ 215 degrees C for both zones and then set the time for 5 minutes to preheat.
4. Rub the steaks with taco seasoning evenly.
5. After preheating, arrange the steak into the basket of each zone.
6. Slide each basket into Air Fryer and set the time for 30 minutes.
7. After cooking time is completed, remove the steaks from Air Fryer and place onto a cutting board for about 10-15 minutes before slicing.
8. With a sharp knife, cut each steak into desired size slices and serve.

Meat And Rice Stuffed Peppers

Servings: 4
Cooking Time: 18 Minutes

Ingredients:

- 340 g lean beef mince
- 110 g lean pork mince
- 60 ml onion, minced
- 1 (425 g) can finely-chopped tomatoes
- 1 teaspoon Worcestershire sauce
- 1 teaspoon barbecue seasoning
- 1 teaspoon honey
- ½ teaspoon dried basil
- 120 ml cooked brown rice
- ½ teaspoon garlic powder
- ½ teaspoon oregano
- ½ teaspoon salt
- 2 small peppers, cut in half, stems removed, deseeded
- Cooking spray

Directions:

1. Preheat the zone 1 air fryer drawer to 182°C and spritz a baking pan with cooking spray.
2. Arrange the beef, pork, and onion in the baking pan and bake in the preheated air fryer drawer for 8 minutes. Break the ground meat into chunks halfway through the cooking.
3. Meanwhile, combine the tomatoes, Worcestershire sauce, barbecue seasoning, honey, and basil in a saucepan. Stir to mix well.
4. Transfer the cooked meat mixture to a large bowl and add the cooked rice, garlic powder, oregano, salt, and 60 ml of the tomato mixture. Stir to mix well.
5. Stuff the pepper halves with the mixture, then arrange the pepper halves in the zone 1 air fryer drawer and air fry for 10 minutes or until the peppers are lightly charred.
6. Serve the stuffed peppers with the remaining tomato sauce on top.

Green Pepper Cheeseburgers

Servings: 4
Cooking Time: 30 Minutes

Ingredients:

- 2 green peppers
- 680 g 85% lean beef mince
- 1 clove garlic, minced
- 1 teaspoon salt
- ½ teaspoon freshly ground black pepper
- 4 slices Cheddar cheese (about 85 g)
- 4 large lettuce leaves

Directions:

1. Preheat the air fryer to 204°C.
2. Arrange the peppers in the drawer of the air fryer. Pausing halfway through the cooking time to turn the peppers, air fry for 20 minutes, or until they are softened and beginning to char. Transfer the peppers to a large bowl and cover with a plate. When cool enough to handle, peel off the skin, remove the seeds and stems, and slice into strips. Set aside.
3. Meanwhile, in a large bowl, combine the beef with the garlic, salt, and pepper. Shape the beef into 4 patties.
4. Lower the heat on the air fryer to 182°C. Arrange the burgers in a single layer in the two drawers of the air fryer. Pausing halfway through the cooking time to turn the burgers, air fry for 10 minutes, or until a thermometer inserted into the thickest part registers 72°C.
5. Top the burgers with the cheese slices and continue baking for a minute or two, just until the cheese has melted. Serve the burgers on a lettuce leaf topped with the roasted peppers.

Mongolian Beef With Sweet Chili Brussels Sprouts

Servings:4
Cooking Time: 20 Minutes

Ingredients:

- FOR THE MONGOLIAN BEEF
- 1 pound flank steak, cut into thin strips
- 1 tablespoon olive oil
- 2 tablespoons cornstarch
- ½ cup reduced-sodium soy sauce
- ½ cup packed light brown sugar
- 1 tablespoon chili paste (optional)
- 1 tablespoon minced garlic
- 1 tablespoon minced fresh ginger
- 2 scallions, chopped
- FOR THE BRUSSELS SPROUTS
- 1 pound Brussels sprouts, halved lengthwise
- 1 tablespoon olive oil
- ½ cup gochujang sauce
- 2 tablespoons rice vinegar
- 1 tablespoon reduced-sodium soy sauce
- 1 tablespoon light brown sugar
- 1 teaspoon fresh garlic

Directions:

1. To prep the Mongolian beef: In a large bowl, combine the flank steak and olive oil and toss to coat. Add the cornstarch and toss to coat.
2. In a small bowl, whisk together the soy sauce, brown sugar, chili paste (if using), garlic, and ginger. Set the soy sauce mixture aside.
3. To prep the Brussels sprouts: In a large bowl, combine the Brussels sprouts and oil and toss to coat.
4. In a small bowl, whisk together the gochujang sauce, vinegar, soy sauce, brown sugar, and garlic. Set the chili sauce mixture aside.
5. To cook the beef and Brussels sprouts: Install a crisper plate in each of the two baskets. Place the beef in the Zone 1 basket and insert the basket in the unit. Place the Brussels sprouts in the Zone 2 basket and insert the basket in the unit.
6. Select Zone 1, select AIR FRY, set the temperature to 390°F, and set the time to 15 minutes.
7. Select Zone 2, select AIR FRY, set the temperature to 400°F, and set the time to 20 minutes. Select SMART FINISH.
8. Press START/PAUSE to begin cooking.
9. When both timers read 5 minutes, press START/PAUSE. Remove the Zone 1 basket, add the reserved soy sauce mixture and the scallions, and toss with the beef. Reinsert the basket. Remove the Zone 2 basket, add the reserved chili sauce mixture, and toss with the Brussels sprouts. Reinsert the basket and press START/PAUSE to resume cooking.
10. When cooking is complete, the steak should be cooked through and the Brussels sprouts tender and slightly caramelized. Serve warm.

Nutrition:

- (Per serving) Calories: 481; Total fat: 16g; Saturated fat: 4.5g; Carbohydrates: 60g; Fiber: 5g; Protein: 27g; Sodium: 2,044mg

Italian-style Meatballs With Garlicky Roasted Broccoli

Servings:4
Cooking Time: 15 Minutes

Ingredients:

- FOR THE MEATBALLS
- 1 large egg
- ¼ cup Italian-style bread crumbs
- 1 pound ground beef (85 percent lean)
- ¼ cup grated Parmesan cheese
- ¼ teaspoon kosher salt
- Nonstick cooking spray
- 2 cups marinara sauce
- FOR THE ROASTED BROCCOLI
- 4 cups broccoli florets
- 1 tablespoon olive oil
- ¼ teaspoon kosher salt
- ¼ teaspoon freshly ground pepper
- ¼ teaspoon red pepper flakes
- 1 tablespoon minced garlic

Directions:

1. To prep the meatballs: In a large bowl, beat the egg. Mix in the bread crumbs and let sit for 5 minutes.
2. Add the beef, Parmesan, and salt and mix until just combined. Form the meatball mixture into 8 meatballs, about 1 inch in diameter. Mist with cooking spray.
3. To prep the broccoli: In a large bowl, combine the broccoli, olive oil, salt, black pepper, and red pepper flakes. Toss to coat the broccoli evenly.
4. To cook the meatballs and broccoli: Install a crisper plate in the Zone 1 basket. Place the meatballs in the basket and insert the basket in the unit. Place the broccoli in the Zone 2 basket, sprinkle the garlic over the broccoli, and insert the basket in the unit.
5. Select Zone 1, select AIR FRY, set the temperature to 400°F, and set the time to 12 minutes.
6. Select Zone 2, select ROAST, set the temperature to 390°F, and set the time to 15 minutes. Select SMART FINISH.
7. Press START/PAUSE to begin cooking.
8. When the Zone 1 timer reads 5 minutes, press START/PAUSE. Remove the basket and pour the marinara sauce over the meatballs. Reinsert the basket and press START/PAUSE to resume cooking.
9. When cooking is complete, the meatballs should be cooked through and the broccoli will have begun to brown on the edges.

Nutrition:

- (Per serving) Calories: 493; Total fat: 33g; Saturated fat: 9g; Carbohydrates: 24g; Fiber: 3g; Protein: 31g; Sodium: 926mg

Pork Tenderloin With Brown Sugar–pecan Sweet Potatoes

Servings:4
Cooking Time: 45 Minutes

Ingredients:

- FOR THE PORK TENDERLOIN
- 1½ pounds pork tenderloin
- 2 teaspoons vegetable oil
- ½ teaspoon kosher salt
- ½ teaspoon poultry seasoning
- FOR THE SWEET POTATOES
- 4 teaspoons unsalted butter, at room temperature
- 2 tablespoons dark brown sugar
- ¼ cup chopped pecans
- 4 small sweet potatoes

Directions:

1. To prep the pork: Coat the pork tenderloin with the oil, then rub with the salt and poultry seasoning.
2. To prep the sweet potatoes: In a small bowl, mix the butter, brown sugar, and pecans until well combined.
3. To cook the pork and sweet potatoes: Install a crisper plate in the Zone 1 basket. Place the pork tenderloin in the basket and insert the basket in the unit. Place the sweet potatoes in the Zone 2 basket and insert the basket in the unit.
4. Select Zone 1, select AIR FRY, set the temperature to 390°F, and set the time to 25 minutes.
5. Select Zone 2, select BAKE, set the temperature to 400°F, and set the time to 45 minutes. Select SMART FINISH.
6. Press START/PAUSE to begin cooking.
7. When the Zone 2 timer reads 10 minutes, press START/PAUSE. Remove the basket. Slice the sweet potatoes open lengthwise. Divide the pecan mixture among the potatoes. Reinsert the basket and press START/PAUSE to resume cooking.
8. When cooking is complete, the pork will be cooked through (an instant-read thermometer should read 145°F) and the potatoes will be soft and their flesh fluffy.
9. Transfer the pork loin to a plate or cutting board and let rest for at least 5 minutes before slicing and serving.

Nutrition:

- (Per serving) Calories: 415; Total fat: 15g; Saturated fat: 4.5g; Carbohydrates: 33g; Fiber: 4.5g; Protein: 36g; Sodium: 284mg

Chipotle Beef

Servings: 4
Cooking Time: 18 Minutes.

Ingredients:

- 1 lb. beef steak, cut into chunks
- 1 large egg
- ½ cup parmesan cheese, grated
- ½ cup pork panko
- ½ teaspoon seasoned salt
- Chipotle Ranch Dip
- ¼ cup mayonnaise
- ¼ cup sour cream
- 1 teaspoon chipotle paste
- ½ teaspoon ranch dressing mix
- ¼ medium lime, juiced

Directions:

1. Mix all the ingredients for chipotle ranch dip in a bowl.
2. Keep it in the refrigerator for 30 minutes.
3. Mix pork panko with salt and parmesan.
4. Beat egg in one bowl and spread the panko mixture in another flat bowl.
5. Dip the steak chunks in the egg first, then coat them with panko mixture.
6. Spread them in the two crisper plates and spray them with cooking oil.
7. Return the crisper plate to the Ninja Foodi Dual Zone Air Fryer.
8. Choose the Air Fry mode for Zone 1 and set the temperature to 390 degrees F and the time to 18 minutes.
9. Select the "MATCH" button to copy the settings for Zone 2.
10. Initiate cooking by pressing the START/STOP button.
11. Serve with chipotle ranch and salt and pepper on top. Enjoy.

Nutrition:

- (Per serving) Calories 310 | Fat 17g |Sodium 271mg | Carbs 4.3g | Fiber 0.9g | Sugar 2.1g | Protein 35g

Easy Breaded Pork Chops

Servings: 8
Cooking Time: 20 Minutes

Ingredients:

- 1 egg
- 118ml milk
- 8 pork chops
- 1 packet ranch seasoning
- 238g breadcrumbs
- Pepper
- Salt

Directions:

1. In a small bowl, whisk the egg and milk.
2. In a separate shallow dish, mix breadcrumbs, ranch seasoning, pepper, and salt.
3. Dip each pork chop in the egg mixture, then coat with breadcrumbs.
4. Insert a crisper plate in the Ninja Foodi air fryer baskets.
5. Place the coated pork chops in both baskets.
6. Select zone 1, then select air fry mode and set the temperature to 360 degrees F for 12 minutes. Press "match" to match zone 2 settings to zone 1. Press "start/stop" to begin. Turn halfway through.

Scallops With Greens

Servings: 8
Cooking Time: 13 Minutes

Ingredients:

- ¾ cup heavy whipping cream
- 1 tablespoon tomato paste
- 1 tablespoon chopped fresh basil
- 1 teaspoon garlic, minced
- ½ teaspoons salt
- ½ teaspoons pepper
- 12 ounces frozen spinach thawed
- 8 jumbo sea scallops
- Vegetable oil to spray

Directions:

1. Season the scallops with vegetable oil, salt, and pepper in a bowl
2. Mix cream with spinach, basil, garlic, salt, pepper, and tomato paste in a bowl.
3. Pour this mixture over the scallops and mix gently.
4. Divide the scallops in the Air Fryers Baskets without using the crisper plate.
5. Return the crisper plate to the Ninja Foodi Dual Zone Air Fryer.
6. Choose the Air Fry mode for Zone 1 and set the temperature to 390 degrees F and the time to 13 minutes|
7. Select the "MATCH" button to copy the settings for Zone 2.
8. Initiate cooking by pressing the START/STOP button.
9. Serve right away

Mustard Pork Chops

Servings: 4
Cooking Time: 15 Minutes

Ingredients:

- 450g pork chops, boneless
- 55g brown mustard
- 85g honey
- 57g mayonnaise
- 34g BBQ sauce
- Pepper
- Salt

Directions:

1. Coat pork chops with mustard, honey, mayonnaise, BBQ sauce, pepper, and salt in a bowl. Cover and place the bowl in the refrigerator for 1 hour.
2. Insert a crisper plate in the Ninja Foodi air fryer baskets.
3. Place the marinated pork chops in both baskets.
4. Select zone 1, then select "bake" mode and set the temperature to 380 degrees F for 15 minutes. Press "match" and then press "start/stop" to begin. Turn halfway through.

Mustard Rubbed Lamb Chops

Servings: 4
Cooking Time: 31 Minutes.

Ingredients:

- 1 teaspoon Dijon mustard
- 1 teaspoon olive oil
- ½ teaspoon soy sauce
- ½ teaspoon garlic, minced
- ½ teaspoon cumin powder
- ½ teaspoon cayenne pepper
- ½ teaspoon Italian spice blend
- ⅛ teaspoon salt
- 4 pieces of lamb chops

Directions:

1. Mix Dijon mustard, soy sauce, olive oil, garlic, cumin powder, cayenne pepper, Italian spice blend, and salt in a medium bowl and mix well.
2. Place lamb chops into a Ziploc bag and pour in the marinade.
3. Press the air out of the bag and seal tightly.
4. Press the marinade around the lamb chops to coat.
5. Keep then in the fridge and marinate for at least 30 minutes, up to overnight.
6. Place 2 chops in each of the crisper plate and spray them with cooking oil.
7. Return the crisper plate to the Ninja Foodi Dual Zone Air Fryer.
8. Select the Roast mode for Zone 1 and set the temperature to 350 degrees F and the time to 27 minutes.
9. Select the "MATCH" button to copy the settings for Zone 2.
10. Initiate cooking by pressing the START/STOP button.
11. Flip the chops once cooked halfway through, and resume cooking.
12. Switch the Roast mode to Max Crisp mode and cook for 5 minutes.
13. Serve warm.

Nutrition:

- (Per serving) Calories 264 | Fat 17g |Sodium 129mg | Carbs 0.9g | Fiber 0.3g | Sugar 0g | Protein 27g

Fish And Seafood Recipes

Cod With Jalapeño

Servings: 4
Cooking Time: 14 Minutes

Ingredients:

- 4 cod fillets, boneless
- 1 jalapeño, minced
- 1 tablespoon avocado oil
- ½ teaspoon minced garlic

Directions:

1. In the shallow bowl, mix minced jalapeño, avocado oil, and minced garlic.
2. Put the cod fillets in the two air fryer drawers in one layer and top with minced jalapeño mixture.
3. Cook the fish at 185°C for 7 minutes per side.

Fried Prawns

Servings: 4

Cooking Time: 5 Minutes

Ingredients:

- 70 g self-raising flour
- 1 teaspoon paprika
- 1 teaspoon salt
- ½ teaspoon freshly ground black pepper
- 1 large egg, beaten
- 120 g finely crushed panko bread crumbs
- 20 frozen large prawns (about 900 g), peeled and deveined
- Cooking spray

Directions:

1. In a shallow bowl, whisk the flour, paprika, salt, and pepper until blended. Add the beaten egg to a second shallow bowl and the bread crumbs to a third.
2. One at a time, dip the prawns into the flour, the egg, and the bread crumbs, coating thoroughly.
3. Preheat the air fryer to 205°C. Line the two air fryer baskets with baking paper.
4. Place the prawns on the baking paper and spritz with oil.
5. Air fry for 2 minutes. Shake the baskets, spritz the prawns with oil, and air fry for 3 minutes more until lightly browned and crispy. Serve hot.

Tilapia With Mojo And Crispy Plantains

Servings:4

Cooking Time: 30 Minutes

Ingredients:

- FOR THE TILAPIA
- 4 tilapia fillets (6 ounces each)
- 2 tablespoons all-purpose flour
- Nonstick cooking spray
- ¼ cup freshly squeezed orange juice
- 3 tablespoons fresh lime juice
- 2 tablespoons olive oil
- 1 tablespoon minced garlic
- ½ teaspoon ground cumin
- ¼ teaspoon kosher salt
- FOR THE PLANTAINS
- 1 large green plantain
- 2 cups cold water
- 2 teaspoons kosher salt
- Nonstick cooking spray

Directions:

1. To prep the tilapia: Dust both sides of the tilapia fillets with the flour, then spritz with cooking spray.
2. In a small bowl, whisk together the orange juice, lime juice, oil, garlic, cumin, and salt. Set the mojo sauce aside.
3. To prep the plantains: Cut the ends from the plantain, then remove and discard the peel. Slice the plantain into 1-inch rounds.
4. In a large bowl, combine the water, salt, and plantains. Let soak for 15 minutes.
5. Drain the plantains and pat them dry with paper towels. Spray with cooking spray.
6. To cook the tilapia and plantains: Install a crisper plate in each of the two baskets. Place the tilapia in a single layer in the Zone 1 basket (work in batches if needed) and insert the basket in the unit. Place the plantains in the Zone 2 basket and insert the basket in the unit.
7. Select Zone 1, select AIR FRY, set the temperature to 390°F, and set the timer to 10 minutes.
8. Select Zone 2, select AIR FRY, set the temperature to 390°F, and set the timer to 30 minutes. Select SMART FINISH.
9. Press START/PAUSE to begin cooking.
10. When the Zone 2 timer reads 10 minutes, press START/PAUSE. Remove the basket and use silicone-tipped tongs to transfer the plantains, which should be tender, to a cutting board. Use the bottom of a heavy glass to smash each plantain flat. Spray both sides with cooking spray and place them back in the basket. Reinsert the basket and press START/PAUSE to resume cooking.
11. When the Zone 1 timer reads 5 minutes, press START/PAUSE. Remove the basket. Spoon half of the mojo sauce over the tilapia. Reinsert the basket and press START/PAUSE to resume cooking.
12. When cooking is complete, the fish should be cooked through and the plantains crispy. Serve the tilapia and plantains with the remaining mojo sauce for dipping.

Nutrition:

- (Per serving) Calories: 380; Total fat: 21g; Saturated fat: 2g; Carbohydrates: 20g; Fiber: 1g; Protein: 35g; Sodium: 217mg

Tuna Patties With Spicy Sriracha Sauce Coconut Prawns

Servings: 6
Cooking Time: 10 Minutes

Ingredients:

- Tuna Patties with Spicy Sriracha Sauce:
- 2 (170 g) cans tuna packed in oil, drained
- 3 tablespoons almond flour
- 2 tablespoons mayonnaise
- 1 teaspoon dried dill
- ½ teaspoon onion powder
- Pinch of salt and pepper
- Spicy Sriracha Sauce:
- 60 g mayonnaise
- 1 tablespoon Sriracha sauce
- 1 teaspoon garlic powder
- Coconut Prawns:
- 230 g medium prawns, peeled and deveined
- 2 tablespoons salted butter, melted
- ½ teaspoon Old Bay seasoning
- 25 g desiccated, unsweetened coconut

Directions:

1. Make the Tuna Patties with Spicy Sriracha Sauce :
2. 1. Preheat the air fryer to 192°C. Line the zone 1 drawer with baking paper. In a large bowl, combine the tuna, almond flour, mayonnaise, dill, and onion powder. Season to taste with salt and freshly ground black pepper. Use a fork to stir, mashing with the back of the fork as necessary, until thoroughly combined. 3. Use an ice cream scoop to form the tuna mixture patties. Place the patties in a single layer on the baking paper in the zone 1 air fryer drawer. Press lightly with the bottom of the scoop to flatten into a circle about ½ inch thick. Pausing halfway through the cooking time to turn the patties, air fry for 10 minutes until lightly browned. 4. To make the Sriracha sauce: In a small bowl, combine the mayonnaise, Sriracha, and garlic powder. Serve the tuna patties topped with the Sriracha sauce.
3. Make the Coconut Prawns :
4. In a large bowl, toss the prawns in butter and Old Bay seasoning.
5. Place shredded coconut in bowl. Coat each piece of prawns in the coconut and place into the zone 2 air fryer drawer.
6. Adjust the temperature to 204°C and air fry for 6 minutes.
7. Gently turn the prawns halfway through the cooking time. Serve immediately.

Lemon Pepper Fish Fillets

Servings: 4
Cooking Time: 10 Minutes

Ingredients:

- 4 tilapia fillets
- 30ml olive oil
- 2 tbsp lemon zest
- ⅛ tsp paprika
- 1 tsp garlic, minced
- 1 ½ tsp ground peppercorns
- Pepper
- Salt

Directions:

1. In a small bowl, mix oil, peppercorns, paprika, garlic, lemon zest, pepper, and salt.
2. Brush the fish fillets with oil mixture.
3. Insert a crisper plate in the Ninja Foodi air fryer baskets.
4. Place fish fillets in both baskets.
5. Select zone 1 then select "air fry" mode and set the temperature to 390 degrees F for 10 minutes. Press "match" to match zone 2 settings to zone 1. Press "start/stop" to begin.

Nutrition:

- (Per serving) Calories 203 | Fat 9g |Sodium 99mg | Carbs 0.9g | Fiber 0.2g | Sugar 0.2g | Protein 32.1g

Basil Cheese Salmon

Servings: 4
Cooking Time:7 Minutes

Ingredients:

- 4 salmon fillets
- 1/4 cup parmesan cheese, grated
- 5 fresh basil leaves, minced
- 2 tbsp mayonnaise
- 1/2 lemon juice
- Pepper
- Salt

Directions:

1. Preheat the air fryer to 400 F.
2. Brush salmon fillets with lemon juice and season with pepper and salt.
3. In a small bowl, mix mayonnaise, basil, and cheese.
4. Spray air fryer basket with cooking spray.
5. Place salmon fillets into the air fryer basket and brush with mayonnaise mixture and cook for 7 minutes.
6. Serve and enjoy.

South Indian Fried Fish

Servings: 4

Cooking Time: 8 Minutes

Ingredients:

- 2 tablespoons olive oil
- 2 tablespoons fresh lime or lemon juice
- 1 teaspoon minced fresh ginger
- 1 clove garlic, minced
- 1 teaspoon ground turmeric
- ½ teaspoon kosher or coarse sea salt
- ¼ to ½ teaspoon cayenne pepper
- 455 g tilapia fillets (2 to 3 fillets)
- Olive oil spray
- Lime or lemon wedges (optional)

Directions:

1. In a large bowl, combine the oil, lime juice, ginger, garlic, turmeric, salt, and cayenne. Stir until well combined; set aside.
2. Cut each tilapia fillet into three or four equal-size pieces. Add the fish to the bowl and gently mix until all of the fish is coated in the marinade. Marinate for 10 to 15 minutes at room temperature.
3. Spray the air fryer basket with olive oil spray. Place the fish in the basket and spray the fish. Set the air fryer to 165°C for 3 minutes to partially cook the fish. Set the air fryer to 205°C for 5 minutes to finish cooking and crisp up the fish.
4. Carefully remove the fish from the basket. Serve hot, with lemon wedges if desired.

Flavorful Salmon With Green Beans

Servings: 4

Cooking Time: 10 Minutes

Ingredients:

- 4 ounces green beans
- 1 tablespoon canola oil
- 4 (6-ounce) salmon fillets
- ⅓ cup prepared sesame-ginger sauce
- Kosher salt, to taste
- Black pepper, to taste

Directions:

1. Toss the green beans with a teaspoon each of salt and pepper in a large bowl.
2. Place a crisper plate in each drawer. Place the green beans in the zone 1 drawer and insert it into the unit. Place the salmon into the zone 2 drawer and place it into the unit.
3. Select zone 1, then AIR FRY, and set the temperature to 390 degrees F/ 200 degrees C with a 10-minute timer.
4. Select zone 2, then AIR FRY, and set the temperature to 390 degrees F/ 200 degrees C with a 15-minute timer. Select SYNC. To begin cooking, press the START/STOP button.
5. Press START/STOP to pause the unit when the zone 2 timer reaches 9 minutes. Remove the salmon from the drawer and toss it in the sesame-ginger sauce. To resume cooking, replace the drawer in the device and press START/STOP.
6. When cooking is complete, serve the salmon and green beans immediately.

Nutrition:

- (Per serving) Calories 305 | Fat 16g | Sodium 535mg | Carbs 8.7g | Fiber 1g | Sugar 6.4g | Protein 34.9g

Spicy Salmon Fillets

Servings: 6

Cooking Time: 8 Minutes

Ingredients:

- 900g salmon fillets
- ¾ tsp ground cumin
- 1 tbsp brown sugar
- 2 tbsp steak seasoning
- ¼ tsp cayenne pepper
- ½ tsp ground coriander

Directions:

1. Mix ground cumin, coriander, steak seasoning, brown sugar, and cayenne in a small bowl.
2. Rub salmon fillets with spice mixture.
3. Insert a crisper plate in the Ninja Foodi air fryer baskets.
4. Place the salmon fillets in both baskets.
5. Select zone 1, then select "bake" mode and set the temperature to 360 degrees F for 10 minutes. Press "match" to match zone 2 settings to zone 1. Press "start/stop" to begin.

Nutrition:

- (Per serving) Calories 207 | Fat 9.4g |Sodium 68mg | Carbs 1.6g | Fiber 0.1g | Sugar 1.5g | Protein 29.4g

Lemon Pepper Salmon With Asparagus

Servings:2
Cooking Time:18

Ingredients:

- 1 cup of green asparagus
- 2 tablespoons of butter
- 2 fillets of salmon, 8 ounces each
- Salt and black pepper, to taste
- 1 teaspoon of lemon juice
- ½ teaspoon of lemon zest
- oil spray, for greasing

Directions:

1. Rinse and trim the asparagus.
2. Rinse and pat dry the salmon fillets.
3. Take a bowl and mix lemon juice, lemon zest, salt, and black pepper.
4. Brush the fish fillet with the rub and place it in the zone 1 basket.
5. Place asparagus in zone 2 basket.
6. Spray the asparagus with oil spray.
7. Set zone 1 to AIRFRY mode for 18 minutes at 390 degrees F.
8. Set the zone 2 to 5 minutes at 390 degrees F, at air fry mode.
9. Hit the smart finish button to finish at the same time.
10. Once done, serve and enjoy.

Nutrition:

- (Per serving) Calories 482| Fat 28g| Sodium209 mg | Carbs 2.8g | Fiber1.5 g | Sugar1.4 g | Protein 56.3g

Cajun Scallops

Servings: 6
Cooking Time: 6 Minutes

Ingredients:

- 6 sea scallops
- Cooking spray
- Salt to taste
- Cajun seasoning

Directions:

1. Season the scallops with Cajun seasoning and salt.
2. Place them in one air fryer basket and spray them with cooking oil.
3. Return the air fryer basket 1 to Zone 1 of the Ninja Foodi 2-Basket Air Fryer.
4. Choose the "Air Fry" mode for Zone 1 and set the temperature to 400 degrees F and 6 minutes of cooking time.
5. Initiate cooking by pressing the START/PAUSE BUTTON.
6. Flip the scallops once cooked halfway through.
7. Serve warm.

Nutrition:

- (Per serving) Calories 266 | Fat 6.3g |Sodium 193mg | Carbs 39.1g | Fiber 7.2g | Sugar 5.2g | Protein 14.8g

Herbed Prawns Pita

Servings: 4
Cooking Time: 8 Minutes

Ingredients:

- 455 g medium prawns, peeled and deveined
- 2 tablespoons olive oil
- 1 teaspoon dried oregano
- ½ teaspoon dried thyme
- ½ teaspoon garlic powder
- ¼ teaspoon onion powder
- ½ teaspoon salt
- ¼ teaspoon black pepper
- 4 whole wheat pitas
- 110 g feta cheese, crumbled
- 75 g shredded lettuce
- 1 tomato, diced
- 45 g black olives, sliced
- 1 lemon

Directions:

1. Preheat the oven to 192°C.
2. In a medium bowl, combine the prawns with the olive oil, oregano, thyme, garlic powder, onion powder, salt, and black pepper.
3. Pour prawns in a single layer in the two air fryer drawers and roast for 6 to 8 minutes, or until cooked through.
4. Remove from the air fryer and divide into warmed pitas with feta, lettuce, tomato, olives, and a squeeze of lemon.

Honey Teriyaki Salmon

Servings: 3
Cooking Time: 12 Minutes

Ingredients:

- 8 tablespoon teriyaki sauce
- 3 tablespoons honey
- 2 cubes frozen garlic
- 2 tablespoons olive oil
- 3 pieces wild salmon

Directions:

1. Mix teriyaki sauce, honey, garlic and oil in a large bowl.
2. Add salmon to this sauce and mix well to coat.
3. Cover and refrigerate the salmon for 20 minutes.
4. Place the salmon pieces in one air fryer basket.
5. Return the air fryer basket 1 to Zone 1 of the Ninja Foodi 2-Basket Air Fryer.
6. Choose the "Air Fry" mode for Zone 1 and set the temperature to 350 degrees F and 12 minutes of cooking time.
7. Initiate cooking by pressing the START/PAUSE BUTTON.
8. Flip the pieces once cooked halfway through.
9. Serve warm.

Nutrition:

- (Per serving) Calories 260 | Fat 16g |Sodium 585mg | Carbs 3.1g | Fiber 1.3g | Sugar 0.2g | Protein 25.5g

Scallops And Spinach With Cream Sauce And Confetti Salmon Burgers

Servings: 6
Cooking Time: 12 Minutes

Ingredients:

- Scallops and Spinach with Cream Sauce:
- Vegetable oil spray
- 280 g frozen spinach, thawed and drained
- 8 jumbo sea scallops
- Kosher or coarse sea salt, and black pepper, to taste
- 180 ml heavy cream
- 1 tablespoon tomato paste
- 1 tablespoon chopped fresh basil
- 1 teaspoon minced garlic
- Confetti Salmon Burgers:
- 400 g cooked fresh or canned salmon, flaked with a fork
- 40 g minced spring onions, white and light green parts only
- 40 g minced red bell pepper
- 40 g minced celery
- 2 small lemons
- 1 teaspoon crab boil seasoning such as Old Bay
- ½ teaspoon kosher or coarse sea salt
- ½ teaspoon black pepper
- 1 egg, beaten
- 30 g fresh bread crumbs
- Vegetable oil, for spraying

Directions:

1. Make the Scallops and Spinach with Cream Sauce :
2. Spray a baking pan with vegetable oil spray. Spread the thawed spinach in an even layer in the bottom of the pan.
3. Spray both sides of the scallops with vegetable oil spray. Season lightly with salt and pepper. Arrange the scallops on top of the spinach.
4. In a small bowl, whisk together the cream, tomato paste, basil, garlic, ½ teaspoon salt, and ½ teaspoon pepper. Pour the sauce over the scallops and spinach.
5. Place the pan in the zone 1 air fryer drawer. Set the temperature to 176°C for 10 minutes. Use a meat thermometer to ensure the scallops have an internal temperature of 56°C.
6. Make the Confetti Salmon Burgers :
7. In a large bowl, combine the salmon, vegetables, the zest and juice of 1 of the lemons, crab boil seasoning, salt, and pepper. Add the egg and bread crumbs and stir to combine. Form the mixture into 4 patties weighing approximately 140 g each. Chill until firm, about 15 minutes.
8. Preheat the 2 air fryer drawer to 204°C.
9. Spray the salmon patties with oil on all sides and spray the zone 2 air fryer drawer to prevent sticking. Air fry for 12 minutes, flipping halfway through, until the burgers are browned and cooked through. Cut the remaining lemon into 4 wedges and serve with the burgers.

Broiled Teriyaki Salmon With Eggplant In Stir-fry Sauce

Servings:4
Cooking Time: 25 Minutes
Ingredients:

- FOR THE TERIYAKI SALMON
- 4 salmon fillets (6 ounces each)
- ½ cup teriyaki sauce
- 3 scallions, sliced
- FOR THE EGGPLANT
- ¼ cup reduced-sodium soy sauce
- ¼ cup packed light brown sugar
- 1 tablespoon minced fresh ginger
- 1 tablespoon minced garlic
- 2 teaspoons sesame oil
- ¼ teaspoon red pepper flakes
- 1 eggplant, peeled and cut into bite-size cubes
- Nonstick cooking spray

Directions:

1. To prep the teriyaki salmon: Brush the top of each salmon fillet with the teriyaki sauce.
2. To prep the eggplant: In a small bowl, whisk together the soy sauce, brown sugar, ginger, garlic, sesame oil, and red pepper flakes. Set the stir-fry sauce aside.
3. Spritz the eggplant cubes with cooking spray.
4. To cook the salmon and eggplant: Install a crisper plate in each of the two baskets. Place the salmon in a single layer in the Zone 1 basket and insert the basket in the unit. Place the eggplant in the Zone 2 basket and insert the basket in the unit.
5. Select Zone 1, select AIR BROIL, set the temperature to 450°F, and set the time to 8 minutes.
6. Select Zone 2, select AIR FRY, set the temperature to 390°F, and set the time to 25 minutes. Select SMART FINISH.
7. Press START/PAUSE to begin cooking.
8. When the Zone 2 timer reads 5 minutes, press START/PAUSE. Remove the basket and pour the stir-fry sauce evenly over the eggplant. Shake or stir to coat the eggplant cubes in the sauce. Reinsert the basket and press START/PAUSE to resume cooking.
9. When cooking is complete, the salmon should be cooked to your liking and the eggplant tender and slightly caramelized. Serve hot.

Nutrition:

- (Per serving) Calories: 499; Total fat: 22g; Saturated fat: 2g; Carbohydrates: 36g; Fiber: 3.5g; Protein: 42g; Sodium: 1,024mg

Snapper Scampi

Servings: 4
Cooking Time: 8 To 10 Minutes
Ingredients:

- 4 skinless snapper or arctic char fillets, 170 g each
- 1 tablespoon olive oil
- 3 tablespoons lemon juice, divided
- ½ teaspoon dried basil
- Pinch salt
- Freshly ground black pepper, to taste
- 2 tablespoons butter
- 2 cloves garlic, minced

Directions:

1. Rub the fish fillets with olive oil and 1 tablespoon of the lemon juice. Sprinkle with the basil, salt, and pepper, and place in the two air fryer drawers.
2. Air fry the fish at 192°C for 7 to 8 minutes or until the fish just flakes when tested with a fork. Remove the fish from the drawers and put on a serving plate. Cover to keep warm.
3. In a baking pan, combine the butter, remaining 2 tablespoons lemon juice, and garlic. Bake in the air fryer for 1 to 2 minutes or until the garlic is sizzling. Pour this mixture over the fish and serve

Blackened Red Snapper

Servings: 4
Cooking Time: 8 To 10 Minutes
Ingredients:

- 1½ teaspoons black pepper
- ¼ teaspoon thyme
- ¼ teaspoon garlic powder
- ⅛ teaspoon cayenne pepper
- 1 teaspoon olive oil
- 4 red snapper fillet portions, skin on, 110 g each
- 4 thin slices lemon
- Cooking spray

Directions:

1. Mix the spices and oil together to make a paste. Rub into both sides of the fish.
2. Spray the two air fryer drawers with nonstick cooking spray and lay snapper steaks in drawers, skin-side down.
3. Place a lemon slice on each piece of fish.
4. Roast at 200°C for 8 to 10 minutes. The fish will not flake when done, but it should be white through the center.

Crumb-topped Sole

Servings: 4
Cooking Time: 7 Minutes
Ingredients:

- 3 tablespoons mayonnaise
- 3 tablespoons Parmesan cheese, grated
- 2 teaspoons mustard seeds
- ¼ teaspoon black pepper
- 4 (170g) sole fillets
- 1 cup soft bread crumbs
- 1 green onion, chopped
- ½ teaspoon ground mustard
- 2 teaspoons butter, melted
- Cooking spray

Directions:

1. Mix mayonnaise with black pepper, mustard seeds, and 2 tablespoons cheese in a bowl.
2. Place 2 sole fillets in each air fryer basket and top them with mayo mixture.
3. Mix breadcrumbs with rest of the ingredients in a bowl.
4. Drizzle this mixture over the sole fillets.
5. Return the air fryer basket 1 to Zone 1, and basket 2 to Zone 2 of the Ninja Foodi 2-Basket Air Fryer.
6. Choose the "Air Fry" mode for Zone 1 and set the temperature to 375 degrees F and 7 minutes of cooking time.
7. Select the "MATCH COOK" option to copy the settings for Zone 2.
8. Initiate cooking by pressing the START/PAUSE BUTTON.
9. Serve warm.

Nutrition:

- (Per serving) Calories 308 | Fat 24g |Sodium 715mg | Carbs 0.8g | Fiber 0.1g | Sugar 0.1g | Protein 21.9g

Dukkah-crusted Halibut

Servings: 2
Cooking Time: 17 Minutes
Ingredients:

- Dukkah:
- 1 tablespoon coriander seeds
- 1 tablespoon sesame seeds
- 1½ teaspoons cumin seeds
- 50 g roasted mixed nuts
- ¼ teaspoon kosher or coarse sea salt
- ¼ teaspoon black pepper
- Fish:
- 2 halibut fillets, 140 g each
- 2 tablespoons mayonnaise
- Vegetable oil spray
- Lemon wedges, for serving

Directions:

1. For the Dukkah: Combine the coriander, sesame seeds, and cumin in a small baking pan. Place the pan in the zone 1 air fryer basket. Set the air fryer to 205°C for 5 minutes. Toward the end of the cooking time, you will hear the seeds popping. Transfer to a plate and let cool for 5 minutes. 2. Transfer the toasted seeds to a food processor or spice grinder and add the mixed nuts. Pulse until coarsely chopped. Add the salt and pepper and stir well.
2. 3. For the fish: Spread each fillet with 1 tablespoon of the mayonnaise. Press a heaping tablespoon of the Dukkah into the mayonnaise on each fillet, pressing lightly to adhere. 4. Spray the zone 2 air fryer basket with vegetable oil spray. Place the fish in the zone 2 basket. Cook for 12 minutes, or until the fish flakes easily with a fork. 5. Serve the fish with lemon wedges.

Fish And Chips

Servings:2
Cooking Time:22
Ingredients:

- 1 pound of potatoes, cut lengthwise
- 1 cup seasoned flour
- 2 eggs, organic
- 1/3 cup buttermilk
- 2 cup seafood fry mix
- ½ cup bread crumbs
- 2 codfish fillet, 6 ounces each
- Oil spray, for greasing

Directions:

1. take a bowl and whisk eggs in it along buttermilk.
2. In a separate bowl mix seafood fry mix and bread crumbs
3. Take a baking tray and spread flour on it
4. Dip the fillets first in egg wash, then in flour, and at the end coat it with breadcrumbs mixture.
5. Put the fish fillet in air fryer zone 1 basket.
6. Grease the fish fillet with oil spray.
7. Set zone 1 to AIR FRY mode at 400 degrees F for 14 minutes.
8. Put potato chip in zone two baskets and lightly grease it with oil spray.
9. Set the zone 2 basket to AIRFRY mode at 400 degrees F for 22 minutes.
10. Hit the smart finish button.
11. Once done, serve and enjoy.

Nutrition:

- (Per serving) Calories 992| Fat 22.3g| Sodium1406 mg | Carbs 153.6g | Fiber 10g | Sugar10 g | Protein 40g

Crusted Cod

Servings: 4
Cooking Time: 13 Minutes

Ingredients:

- 2 lbs. cod fillets
- Salt, to taste
- Freshly black pepper, to taste
- ½ cup all-purpose flour
- 1 large egg, beaten
- 2 cups panko bread crumbs
- 1 teaspoon Old Bay seasoning
- Lemon wedges, for serving
- Tartar sauce, for serving

Directions:

1. Rub the fish with salt and black pepper.
2. Add flour in one shallow bowl, beat eggs in another bowl, and mix panko with Old Bay in a shallow bowl.
3. First coat the fish with flour, then dip it in the eggs and finally coat it with the panko mixture.
4. Place half of the seasoned codfish in each crisper plate.
5. Return the crisper plates to the Ninja Foodi Dual Zone Air Fryer.
6. Choose the Air Fry mode for Zone 1 and set the temperature to 390 degrees F and the time to 13 minutes|
7. Select the "MATCH" button to copy the settings for Zone 2.
8. Initiate cooking by pressing the START/STOP button.
9. Flip the fish once cooked halfway, then resume cooking.
10. Serve warm and fresh with tartar sauce and lemon wedges.

Beer Battered Fish Fillet

Servings:2
Cooking Time:14

Ingredients:

- 1 cup all-purpose flour
- 4 tablespoons cornstarch
- 1 teaspoon baking soda
- 8 ounces beer
- 2 egg beaten
- ½ cup all-purpose flour
- 1 teaspoon smoked paprika
- 1 teaspoon salt
- 1/4 teaspoon freshly ground black pepper
- ¼ teaspoon of cayenne pepper
- 2 cod fillets, 1½-inches thick, cut into 4 pieces
- Oil spray, for greasing

Directions:

1. Take a large bowl and combine flour, baking soda, corn starch, and salt
2. In a separate bowl beat eggs along with the beer.
3. In a shallow dish mix paprika, salt, pepper, and cayenne pepper.
4. Dry the codfish fillets with a paper towel.
5. Dip the fish into the eggs and coat it with seasoned flour.
6. Then dip it in the seasoning.
7. Grease the fillet with oil spray.
8. Divide the fillet between both zones.
9. Set zone 1 to AIR FRY mode at 400 degrees F for 14 minutes.
10. Select MACTH button for zone 2 basket.
11. Press start and let the AIR fry do its magic.
12. Once cooking is done, serve the fish.
13. Enjoy it hot.

Nutrition:

- (Per serving) Calories 1691| Fat 6.1g| Sodium 3976mg | Carbs105.1 g | Fiber 3.4g | Sugar15.6 g | Protein 270g

Chili Honey Salmon

Servings: 2
Cooking Time:12 Minutes

Ingredients:

- 2 salmon fillets
- 3 tbsp honey
- 1/2 tbsp chili flakes
- 1/2 tsp chili powder
- 1/2 tsp turmeric
- 1 tsp ground coriander
- 1/8 tsp pepper
- 1/8 tsp salt

Directions:

1. Add honey to microwave-safe bowl and heat for 10 seconds.
2. Add chili flakes, chili powder, turmeric, coriander, pepper, and salt into the honey and mix well.
3. Brush salmon fillets with honey mixture.
4. Place salmon fillets into the air fryer basket and cook at 400 F for 12 minutes.
5. Serve and enjoy.

Salmon Nuggets

Servings: 4
Cooking Time: 15 Minutes
Ingredients:

- ⅓ cup maple syrup
- ¼ teaspoon dried chipotle pepper
- 1 pinch sea salt
- 1 ½ cups croutons
- 1 large egg
- 1 (1 pound) skinless salmon fillet, cut into 1 ½-inch chunk
- cooking spray

Directions:

1. Mix chipotle powder, maple syrup, and salt in a saucepan and cook on a simmer for 5 minutes|
2. Crush the croutons in a food processor and transfer to a bowl.
3. Beat egg in another shallow bowl.
4. Season the salmon chunks with sea salt.
5. Dip the salmon in the egg, then coat with breadcrumbs.
6. Divide the coated salmon chunks in the two crisper plates.
7. Return the crisper plate to the Ninja Foodi Dual Zone Air Fryer.
8. Select the Air Fry mode for Zone 1 and set the temperature to 390 degrees F and the time to 10 minutes|
9. Press the "MATCH" button to copy the settings for Zone 2.
10. Initiate cooking by pressing the START/STOP button.
11. Flip the chunks once cooked halfway through, then resume cooking.
12. Pour the maple syrup on top and serve warm.

Simple Buttery Cod & Salmon On Bed Of Fennel And Carrot

Servings: 4
Cooking Time: 13 To 14 Minutes
Ingredients:

- Simple Buttery Cod:
- 2 cod fillets, 110 g each
- 2 tablespoons salted butter, melted
- 1 teaspoon Old Bay seasoning
- ½ medium lemon, sliced
- Salmon on Bed of Fennel and Carrot:
- 1 fennel bulb, thinly sliced
- 1 large carrot, peeled and sliced
- 1 small onion, thinly sliced
- 60 ml low-fat sour cream
- ¼ teaspoon coarsely ground pepper
- 2 salmon fillets, 140 g each

Directions:

1. Make the Simple Buttery Cod :
2. Place cod fillets into a round baking dish. Brush each fillet with butter and sprinkle with Old Bay seasoning. Lay two lemon slices on each fillet. Cover the dish with foil and place into the zone 1 air fryer basket.
3. Adjust the temperature to 175°C and bake for 8 minutes. Flip halfway through the cooking time. When cooked, internal temperature should be at least 65°C. Serve warm.
4. Make the Salmon on Bed of Fennel and Carrot :
5. Combine the fennel, carrot, and onion in a bowl and toss.
6. Put the vegetable mixture into a baking pan. Roast in the zone 2 air fryer basket at 205°C for 4 minutes or until the vegetables are crisp-tender.
7. Remove the pan from the air fryer. Stir in the sour cream and sprinkle the vegetables with the pepper.
8. Top with the salmon fillets.
9. Return the pan to the air fryer. Roast for another 9 to 10 minutes or until the salmon just barely flakes when tested with a fork.

Perfect Parmesan Salmon

Servings: 4
Cooking Time:10 Minutes
Ingredients:

- 4 salmon fillets
- 1/4 cup parmesan cheese, shredded
- 1/4 tsp dried dill
- 1/2 tbsp Dijon mustard
- 4 tbsp mayonnaise
- 1 lemon juice
- Pepper
- Salt

Directions:

1. In a small bowl, mix cheese, dill, mustard, mayonnaise, lemon juice, pepper, and salt.
2. Place salmon fillets into the air fryer basket and brush with cheese mixture.
3. Cook salmon fillets at 400 F for 10 minutes.
4. Serve and enjoy.

Butter-wine Baked Salmon

Servings: 4
Cooking Time: 10 Minutes

Ingredients:

- 4 tablespoons butter, melted
- 2 cloves garlic, minced
- Sea salt and ground black pepper, to taste
- 60 ml dry white wine or apple cider vinegar
- 1 tablespoon lime juice
- 1 teaspoon smoked paprika
- ½ teaspoon onion powder
- 4 salmon steaks
- Cooking spray

Directions:

1. Place all the ingredients except the salmon and oil in a shallow dish and stir to mix well.
2. Add the salmon steaks, turning to coat well on both sides. Transfer the salmon to the refrigerator to marinate for 30 minutes.
3. Preheat the air fryer to 182ºC.
4. Place the salmon steaks in the two air fryer drawers, discarding any excess marinade. Spray the salmon steaks with cooking spray.
5. Air fry for about 10 minutes, flipping the salmon steaks halfway through, or until cooked to your preferred doneness.
6. Divide the salmon steaks among four plates and serve.

Crusted Shrimp

Servings: 4
Cooking Time: 13 Minutes

Ingredients:

- 1 lb. shrimp
- ½ cup flour, all-purpose
- 1 teaspoon salt
- ½ teaspoon baking powder
- ⅔ cup water
- 2 cups coconut shred
- ½ cup bread crumbs

Directions:

1. In a small bowl, whisk together flour, salt, water, and baking powder. Set aside for 5 minutes|
2. In another shallow bowl, toss bread crumbs with coconut shreds together.
3. Dredge shrimp in liquid, then coat in coconut mixture, making sure it's totally covered.
4. Repeat until all shrimp are coated.
5. Spread half of the shrimp in each crisper plate and spray them with cooking oil.
6. Return the crisper plates to the Ninja Foodi Dual Zone Air Fryer.
7. Choose the Air Fry mode for Zone 1 and set the temperature to 390 degrees F and the time to 13 minutes|
8. Select the "MATCH" button to copy the settings for Zone 2.
9. Initiate cooking by pressing the START/STOP button.
10. Shake the baskets once cooked halfway, then resume cooking.
11. Serve with your favorite dip.

Chili Lime Tilapia

Servings: 4
Cooking Time: 10 Minutes

Ingredients:

- 340g tilapia fillets
- 2 teaspoons chili powder
- 1 teaspoon cumin
- 1 teaspoon garlic powder
- ½ teaspoon oregano
- ½ teaspoon sea salt
- ¼ teaspoon black pepper
- Lime zest from 1 lime
- Juice of ½ lime

Directions:

1. Mix chili powder and other spices with lime juice and zest in a bowl.
2. Rub this spice mixture over the tilapia fillets.
3. Place two fillets in each air basket.
4. Return the air fryer basket to the Ninja Foodi 2 Baskets Air Fryer.
5. Choose the "Air Fry" mode for Zone 1 at 400 degrees F and 10 minutes of cooking time.
6. Select the "MATCH COOK" option to copy the settings for Zone 2.
7. Initiate cooking by pressing the START/PAUSE BUTTON.
8. Flip the tilapia fillets once cooked halfway through.
9. Serve warm.

Nutrition:

- (Per serving) Calories 275 | Fat 1.4g |Sodium 582mg | Carbs 31.5g | Fiber 1.1g | Sugar 0.1g | Protein 29.8g

Stuffed Mushrooms With Crab

Servings: 4
Cooking Time: 18 Minutes

Ingredients:

- 907g baby bella mushrooms
- cooking spray
- 2 teaspoons tony chachere's salt blend
- ¼ red onion, diced
- 2 celery ribs, diced
- 227g lump crab
- ½ cup seasoned bread crumbs
- 1 large egg
- ½ cup parmesan cheese, shredded
- 1 teaspoon oregano
- 1 teaspoon hot sauce

Directions:

1. Mix all the ingredients except the mushrooms in a bowl.
2. Divide the crab filling into the mushroom caps.
3. Place the caps in the air fryer baskets.
4. Return the air fryer basket 1 to Zone 1, and basket 2 to Zone 2 of the Ninja Foodi 2-Basket Air Fryer.
5. Choose the "Air Fry" mode for Zone 1 at 400 degrees F and 18 minutes of cooking time.
6. Select the "MATCH COOK" option to copy the settings for Zone 2.
7. Initiate cooking by pressing the START/PAUSE BUTTON.
8. Serve warm.

Nutrition:

- (Per serving) Calories 399 | Fat 16g |Sodium 537mg | Carbs 28g | Fiber 3g | Sugar 10g | Protein 35g

Two-way Salmon

Servings:2
Cooking Time:18

Ingredients:

- 2 salmon fillets, 8 ounces each
- 2 tablespoons of Cajun seasoning
- 2 tablespoons of jerk seasoning
- 1 lemon cut in half
- oil spray, for greasing

Directions:

1. First, drizzle lemon juice over the salmon and wash it with tap water.
2. Rinse and pat dry the fillets with a paper towel.
3. Now rub o fillet with Cajun seasoning and grease it with oil spray.
4. Take the second fillet and rub it with jerk seasoning.
5. Grease the second fillet of salmon with oil spray.
6. now put the salmon fillets in both the baskets.
7. Set the Zone 1 basket to 390 degrees F for 16-18 minutes
8. Select MATCH button for zone 2 basket.
9. hit the start button to start cooking.
10. Once the cooking is done, serve the fish hot with mayonnaise.

Nutrition:

- (Per serving) Calories 238| Fat 11.8g| Sodium 488mg | Carbs 9g | Fiber 0g | Sugar8 g | Protein 35g

Crispy Fish Nuggets

Servings: 4
Cooking Time: 8 Minutes

Ingredients:

- 2 eggs
- 96g all-purpose flour
- 700g cod fish fillets, cut into pieces
- 1 tsp garlic powder
- 1 tbsp old bay seasoning
- Pepper
- Salt

Directions:

1. In a small bowl, whisk eggs.
2. Mix flour, garlic powder, old bay seasoning, pepper, and salt in a shallow dish.
3. Coat each fish piece with flour, then dip in egg and again coat with flour.
4. Insert a crisper plate in the Ninja Foodi air fryer baskets.
5. Place coated fish pieces in both baskets.
6. Select zone 1, then select "air fry" mode and set the temperature to 380 degrees F for 8 minutes. Press "match" to match zone 2 settings to zone 1. Press "start/stop" to begin.

Nutrition:

- (Per serving) Calories 298 | Fat 3.9g |Sodium 683mg | Carbs 18.6g | Fiber 0.7g | Sugar 0.4g | Protein 44.1g

Sesame Honey Salmon

Servings: 4
Cooking Time: 10minutes
Ingredients:

- 4 salmon fillets
- 85g honey
- 15ml sesame oil
- 1 tbsp garlic, minced
- 2 tbsp soy sauce
- 1 tbsp sriracha
- Pepper
- Salt

Directions:

1. In a bowl, coat fish fillets with oil, garlic, honey, sriracha, soy sauce, pepper, and salt. Cover and place in refrigerator for 30 minutes.
2. Insert a crisper plate in the Ninja Foodi air fryer baskets.
3. Place the marinated fish fillets in both baskets.
4. Select zone 1, then select "air fry" mode and set the temperature to 375 degrees F for 10 minutes. Press "match" to match zone 2 settings to zone 1. Press "start/stop" to begin.

Nutrition:

- (Per serving) Calories 341 | Fat 14.4g |Sodium 596mg | Carbs 19.5g | Fiber 0.2g | Sugar 17.6g | Protein 35.2g

Southwestern Fish Fillets

Servings: 4
Cooking Time: 16 Minutes
Ingredients:

- 455g trout fillets
- 1 tsp garlic powder
- 29g breadcrumbs
- 15ml olive oil
- 1 tsp chilli powder
- 1 tsp onion powder

Directions:

1. In a small bowl, mix breadcrumbs, garlic powder, onion powder, and chilli powder.
2. Brush fish fillets with oil and coat with breadcrumbs.
3. Insert a crisper plate in the Ninja Foodi air fryer baskets.
4. Place coated fish fillets in both baskets.
5. Select zone 1 then select "air fry" mode and set the temperature to 375 degrees F for 16 minutes. Press "match" and "start/stop" to begin.

Nutrition:

- (Per serving) Calories 272 | Fat 13.5g |Sodium 120mg | Carbs 5g | Fiber 0.6g | Sugar 0.7g | Protein 31.1g

Parmesan-crusted Fish Sticks With Baked Macaroni And Cheese

Servings:4
Cooking Time: 25 Minutes
Ingredients:

- FOR THE FISH STICKS
- 1 pound cod or haddock fillets
- ½ cup all-purpose flour
- 2 large eggs
- ¼ teaspoon kosher salt
- ¼ teaspoon freshly ground black pepper
- ¾ cup panko bread crumbs
- ¼ cup grated Parmesan cheese
- Nonstick cooking spray
- FOR THE MACARONI AND CHEESE
- 1½ cups elbow macaroni
- 1 cup whole milk
- ½ cup heavy (whipping) cream
- 8 ounces shredded Colby-Jack cheese
- 4 ounces cream cheese, at room temperature
- 1 teaspoon Dijon mustard
- ½ teaspoon kosher salt
- ½ teaspoon freshly ground black pepper

Directions:

1. To prep the fish sticks: Cut the fish into sticks about 3 inches long and ¾ inch wide.
2. Set up a breading station with three small shallow bowls. Place the flour in the first bowl. In the second bowl, whisk the eggs and season with the salt and black pepper. Combine the panko and Parmesan in the third bowl.
3. Bread the fish sticks in this order: First, dip them into the flour, coating all sides. Then, dip into the beaten egg. Finally, coat them in the panko mixture, gently pressing the bread crumbs into the fish. Spritz each fish stick all over with cooking spray.
4. To prep the macaroni and cheese: Place the macaroni in the Zone 2 basket. Add the milk, cream, Colby-Jack, cream cheese, mustard, salt, and black pepper. Stir well to combine, ensuring the pasta is completely submerged in the liquid.

5. To cook the fish sticks and macaroni and cheese: Install a crisper plate in the Zone 1 basket. Arrange the fish sticks in a single layer in the basket (use a rack or cook in batches if necessary) and insert the basket in the unit. Insert the Zone 2 basket in the unit.
6. Select Zone 1, select AIR FRY, set the temperature to 390°F, and set the timer to 18 minutes.
7. Select Zone 2, select BAKE, set the temperature to 360°F, and set the timer to 25 minutes. Select SMART FINISH.
8. Press START/PAUSE to begin cooking.
9. When the Zone 1 timer reads 3 minutes, press START/PAUSE. Remove the basket and use silicone-tipped tongs to gently flip over the fish sticks. Reinsert the basket and press START/PAUSE to resume cooking.
10. When cooking is complete, the fish sticks should be crisp and the macaroni tender.
11. Stir the macaroni and cheese and let stand for 5 minutes before serving. The sauce will thicken as it cools.

Nutrition:

- (Per serving) Calories: 903; Total fat: 51g; Saturated fat: 25g; Carbohydrates: 60g; Fiber: 2.5g; Protein: 48g; Sodium: 844mg

Cod With Avocado And Garlic Prawns

Servings: 5
Cooking Time: 10 Minutes

Ingredients:

- Cod with Avocado:
- 90 g shredded cabbage
- 60 ml full-fat sour cream
- 2 tablespoons full-fat mayonnaise
- 20 g chopped pickled jalapeños
- 2 (85 g) cod fillets
- 1 teaspoon chilli powder
- 1 teaspoon cumin
- ½ teaspoon paprika
- ¼ teaspoon garlic powder
- 1 medium avocado, peeled, pitted, and sliced
- ½ medium lime
- Garlic Prawns:
- Prawns:
- Olive or vegetable oil, for spraying
- 450 g medium raw prawns, peeled and deveined
- 6 tablespoons unsalted butter, melted
- 120 g panko bread crumbs
- 2 tablespoons garlic granules
- 1 teaspoon salt
- ½ teaspoon freshly ground black pepper
- Garlic Butter Sauce:
- 115 g unsalted butter
- 2 teaspoons garlic granules
- ¾ teaspoon salt (omit if using salted butter)

Directions:

1. Make the Cod with Avocado :
2. In a large bowl, place cabbage, sour cream, mayonnaise, and jalapeños. Mix until fully coated. Let sit for 20 minutes in the refrigerator.
3. Sprinkle cod fillets with chilli powder, cumin, paprika, and garlic powder. Place each fillet into the zone 1 air fryer drawer.
4. Adjust the temperature to 188°C and set the timer for 10 minutes.
5. Flip the fillets halfway through the cooking time. When fully cooked, fish should have an internal temperature of at least 64°C.
6. To serve, divide slaw mixture into two serving bowls, break cod fillets into pieces and spread over the bowls, and top with avocado. Squeeze lime juice over each bowl. Serve immediately.
7. Make the Garlic Prawns :
8. Make the Prawns
9. Preheat the air fryer to 204°C. Line the zone 2 air fryer drawer with baking paper and spray lightly with oil.
10. Place the prawns and melted butter in a zip-top plastic bag, seal, and shake well, until evenly coated.
11. In a medium bowl, mix together the breadcrumbs, garlic, salt, and black pepper.
12. Add the prawns to the panko mixture and toss until evenly coated. Shake off any excess coating.
13. Place the prawns in the prepared drawer and spray lightly with oil.
14. Cook for 8 to 10 minutes, flipping and spraying with oil after 4 to 5 minutes, until golden brown and crispy. Make the Garlic Butter Sauce
15. In a microwave-safe bowl, combine the butter, garlic, and salt and microwave on 50% power for 30 to 60 seconds, stirring every 15 seconds, until completely melted.
16. Serve the prawns immediately with the garlic butter sauce on the side for dipping.

Prawn Dejonghe Skewers

Servings: 4
Cooking Time: 15 Minutes

Ingredients:

- 2 teaspoons sherry, or apple cider vinegar
- 3 tablespoons unsalted butter, melted
- 120 g panko bread crumbs
- 3 cloves garlic, minced
- 8 g minced flat-leaf parsley, plus more for garnish
- 1 teaspoon kosher salt
- Pinch of cayenne pepper
- 680 g prawns, peeled and deveined
- Vegetable oil, for spraying
- Lemon wedges, for serving

Directions:

1. Stir the sherry and melted butter together in a shallow bowl or pie plate and whisk until combined. Set aside. Whisk together the panko, garlic, parsley, salt, and cayenne pepper on a large plate or shallow bowl.
2. Thread the prawns onto metal skewers designed for the air fryer or bamboo skewers, 3 to 4 per skewer. Dip 1 prawns skewer in the butter mixture, then dredge in the panko mixture until each prawns is lightly coated. Place the skewer on a plate or rimmed baking sheet and repeat the process with the remaining skewers.
3. Preheat the air fryer to 175°C. Arrange 4 skewers in the zone 1 air fryer basket. Spray the skewers with oil and air fry for 8 minutes, until the bread crumbs are golden brown and the prawns are cooked through. Transfer the cooked skewers to a serving plate and keep warm while cooking the remaining 4 skewers in the air fryer.
4. Sprinkle the cooked skewers with additional fresh parsley and serve with lemon wedges if desired.

Crispy Parmesan Cod

Servings: 2
Cooking Time: 10 Minutes

Ingredients:

- 455g cod filets
- Salt and black pepper, to taste
- ½ cup flour
- 2 large eggs, beaten
- ½ teaspoon salt
- 1 cup Panko
- ½ cup grated parmesan
- 2 teaspoons old bay seasoning
- ½ teaspoon garlic powder
- Olive oil spray

Directions:

1. Rub the cod fillets with black pepper and salt.
2. Mix panko with parmesan cheese, old bay seasoning, and garlic powder in a bowl.
3. Mix flour with salt in another bowl.
4. Dredge the cod filets in the flour then dip in the eggs and coat with the Panko mixture.
5. Place the cod fillets in the air fryer baskets.
6. Return the air fryer basket 1 to Zone 1, and basket 2 to Zone 2 of the Ninja Foodi 2-Basket Air Fryer.
7. Choose the "Air Fry" mode for Zone 1 and set the temperature to 400 degrees F and 10 minutes of cooking time.
8. Select the "MATCH COOK" option to copy the settings for Zone 2.
9. Initiate cooking by pressing the START/PAUSE BUTTON.
10. Flip the cod fillets once cooked halfway through.
11. Serve warm.

Nutrition:

- (Per serving) Calories 275 | Fat 1.4g |Sodium 582mg | Carbs 31.5g | Fiber 1.1g | Sugar 0.1g | Protein 29.8g

Frozen Breaded Fish Fillet

Servings:2
Cooking Time:12

Ingredients:

- 4 Frozen Breaded Fish Fillet
- Oil spray, for greasing
- 1 cup mayonnaise

Directions:

1. Take the frozen fish fillets out of the bag and place them in both baskets of the air fryer.
2. Lightly grease it with oil spray.
3. Set the Zone 1 basket to 380 degrees F fo12 minutes.
4. Select the MATCH button for the zone 2 basket.
5. hit the start button to start cooking.
6. Once the cooking is done, serve the fish hot with mayonnaise.

Nutrition:

- (Per serving) Calories 921| Fat 61.5g| Sodium 1575mg | Carbs 69g | Fiber 2g | Sugar 9.5g | Protein 29.1g

Spice-rubbed Chicken Pieces

Servings:6
Cooking Time:40

Ingredients:

- 3 pounds chicken, pieces
- 1 teaspoon sweet paprika
- 1 teaspoon mustard powder
- 1 tablespoon brown sugar, dark
- Salt and black pepper, to taste
- 1 teaspoon Chile powder, New Mexico
- 1 teaspoon oregano, dried
- ¼ teaspoon allspice powder, ground

Directions:

1. Take a bowl and mix dark brown sugar, salt, paprika, mustard powder, oregano, Chile powder, black pepper, and all spice powder.
2. Mix well and rub this spice mixture all over the chicken.
3. Divide the chicken between two air fryer baskets.
4. Oil sprays the meat and then adds it to the air fryer.
5. Now press button1 and button 2 and set the time to 40 minutes at 350 degrees F.
6. Now press start and once the cooking cycle completes, press pause for both the zones.
7. Take out the chicken and serve hot.

Nutrition:

- (Per serving) Calories353 | Fat 7.1g| Sodium400 mg | Carbs 2.2g | Fiber0.4 g | Sugar 1.6g | Protein66 g

Chicken Fajitas With Street Corn

Servings: 4
Cooking Time: 20 Minutes

Ingredients:

- FOR THE FAJITAS
- 1½ pounds boneless, skinless chicken breasts, cut into strips
- 2 bell peppers (red, orange, yellow, or a combination), sliced into ½-inch-wide strips
- 1 small red onion, sliced
- 1 tablespoon vegetable oil
- 2 teaspoons chili powder
- 1 teaspoon ground cumin
- 1 teaspoon kosher salt
- ½ teaspoon freshly ground black pepper
- ½ teaspoon paprika
- ¼ cup fresh cilantro, chopped
- Juice of 1 lime
- 8 (6-inch) flour tortillas
- FOR THE CORN
- ¼ cup mayonnaise
- ¼ cup sour cream
- ¼ cup crumbled Cotija or feta cheese
- 2 tablespoons chopped fresh cilantro
- 1 teaspoon minced garlic
- ½ teaspoon chili powder
- 4 ears corn, husked

Directions:

1. To prep the fajitas: In a large bowl, combine the chicken, bell peppers, onion, oil, chili powder, cumin, salt, black pepper, and paprika and toss to coat.
2. To prep the corn: In a shallow dish, combine the mayonnaise, sour cream, cheese, cilantro, garlic, and chili powder. Mix well and set aside.
3. To cook the fajitas and corn: Install a crisper plate in each of the two baskets. Place the fajita filling in the Zone 1 basket and insert the basket in the unit. Place the corn ears in the Zone 2 basket and insert the basket in the unit.
4. Select Zone 1, select AIR FRY, set the temperature to 390°F, and set the time to 20 minutes.
5. Select Zone 2, select AIR BROIL, set the temperature to 450°F, and set the time to 12 minutes. Select SMART FINISH.
6. Press START/PAUSE to begin cooking.
7. When both timers read 6 minutes, press START/PAUSE. Remove the Zone 1 basket, shake to redistribute the fajita filling, and reinsert the basket. Remove the Zone 2 basket and use silicone-tipped tongs to flip the corn. Reinsert the basket and press START/PAUSE to resume cooking.
8. When cooking is complete, the chicken will be fully cooked and the vegetables will be slightly charred.
9. Mix the cilantro and lime juice into the fajita filling. Divide the filling among the tortillas. Roll the corn in the mayonnaise and cheese mixture to coat. Serve hot.

Chicken Potatoes

Servings: 4
Cooking Time: 22 Minutes

Ingredients:

- 15 ounces canned potatoes drained
- 1 teaspoon olive oil
- 1 teaspoon Lawry's seasoned salt
- ⅛ teaspoons black pepper optional
- 8 ounces boneless chicken breast cubed
- ¼ teaspoon paprika
- ⅜ cup cheddar, shredded
- 4 bacon slices, cooked, cut into strips

Directions:

1. Dice the chicken into small pieces and toss them with olive oil and spices.
2. Drain and dice the potato pieces into smaller cubes.
3. Add potato to the chicken and mix well to coat.
4. Spread the mixture in the two crisper plates in a single layer.
5. Return the crisper plates to the Ninja Foodi Dual Zone Air Fryer.
6. Choose the Air Fry mode for Zone 1 and set the temperature to 390 degrees F and the time to 22 minutes|
7. Select the "MATCH" button to copy the settings for Zone 2.
8. Initiate cooking by pressing the START/STOP button.
9. Top the chicken and potatoes with cheese and bacon.
10. Return the crisper plates to the Ninja Foodi Dual Zone Air Fryer.
11. Select the Max Crisp mode for Zone 1 and set the temperature to 300 degrees F and the time to 5 minutes|
12. Initiate cooking by pressing the START/STOP button.
13. Repeat the same step for Zone 2 to broil the potatoes and chicken in the right drawer.
14. Enjoy with dried herbs on top.

Simply Terrific Turkey Meatballs

Servings: 4
Cooking Time: 7 To 10 Minutes

Ingredients:

- 1 red bell pepper, seeded and coarsely chopped
- 2 cloves garlic, coarsely chopped
- 15 g chopped fresh parsley
- 680 g 85% lean turkey mince
- 1 egg, lightly beaten
- 45 g grated Parmesan cheese
- 1 teaspoon salt
- ½ teaspoon freshly ground black pepper

Directions:

1. Preheat the air fryer to 200°C.
2. In a food processor fitted with a metal blade, combine the bell pepper, garlic, and parsley. Pulse until finely chopped. Transfer the vegetables to a large mixing bowl.
3. Add the turkey, egg, Parmesan, salt, and black pepper. Mix gently until thoroughly combined. Shape the mixture into 1¼-inch meatballs.
4. Arrange the meatballs in a single layer in the two air fryer drawers; coat lightly with olive oil spray. Pausing halfway through the cooking time to shake the drawer, air fry for 7 to 10 minutes, until lightly browned and a thermometer inserted into the centre of a meatball registers 76°C.

Honey Butter Chicken

Servings: 4
Cooking Time: 15 Minutes

Ingredients:

- 4 chicken breasts, boneless
- 85g honey
- 28g butter, melted
- 2 tsp lemon juice
- 15ml olive oil
- 62g Dijon mustard
- Pepper
- Salt

Directions:

1. In a small bowl, mix butter, oil, lemon juice, honey, mustard, pepper, and salt.
2. Insert a crisper plate in the Ninja Foodi air fryer baskets.
3. Brush chicken breasts with butter mixture and place them in both baskets.
4. Select zone 1 then select "bake" mode and set the temperature to 380 degrees F for 15 minutes. Press "match" to match zone 2 settings to zone 1. Press "start/stop" to begin.

Nutrition:

- (Per serving) Calories 434 | Fat 20.7g |Sodium 384mg | Carbs 18.4g | Fiber 0.6g | Sugar 17.6g | Protein 43.1g

Chicken And Vegetable Fajitas

Servings: 6

Cooking Time: 23 Minutes

Ingredients:

- Chicken:
- 450 g boneless, skinless chicken thighs, cut crosswise into thirds
- 1 tablespoon vegetable oil
- 4½ teaspoons taco seasoning
- Vegetables:
- 50 g sliced onion
- 150 g sliced bell pepper
- 1 or 2 jalapeños, quartered lengthwise
- 1 tablespoon vegetable oil
- ½ teaspoon kosher salt
- ½ teaspoon ground cumin
- For Serving:
- Tortillas
- Sour cream
- Shredded cheese
- Guacamole
- Salsa

Directions:

1. For the chicken: In a medium bowl, toss together the chicken, vegetable oil, and taco seasoning to coat. 2. For the vegetables: In a separate bowl, toss together the onion, bell pepper, jalapeño, vegetable oil, salt, and cumin to coat. 3. Place the chicken in the air fryer basket. Set the air fryer to (190°C for 10 minutes. Add the vegetables to the basket, toss everything together to blend the seasonings, and set the air fryer for 13 minutes more. Use a meat thermometer to ensure the chicken has reached an internal temperature of 75°C. 4. Transfer the chicken and vegetables to a serving platter. Serve with tortillas and the desired fajita fixings.

Whole Chicken

Servings: 8

Cooking Time: 20 Minutes

Ingredients:

- 1 whole chicken (about 2.8 pounds), cut in half
- 4 tablespoons olive oil
- 2 teaspoons paprika
- 1 teaspoon garlic powder
- 1 teaspoon onion powder
- Salt and pepper, to taste

Directions:

1. Mix the olive oil, paprika, garlic powder, and onion powder together in a bowl.
2. Place the chicken halves, breast side up, on a plate. Spread a teaspoon or two of the oil mix all over the halves using either your hands or a brush. Season with salt and pepper.
3. Flip the chicken halves over and repeat on the other side. You'll want to reserve a little of the oil mix for later, but other than that, use it liberally.
4. Install a crisper plate in both drawers. Place one half of the chicken in the zone 1 drawer and the other half in the zone 2 drawer, then insert the drawers into the unit.
5. Select zone 1, select AIR FRY, set temperature to 390 degrees F/ 200 degrees C, and set time to 20 minutes. Select MATCH to match zone 2 settings to zone 1. Press the START/STOP button to begin cooking.
6. When cooking is done, check the internal temperature of the chicken. It should read 165°F. If the chicken isn't done, add more cooking time.

Nutrition:

- (Per serving) Calories 131 | Fat 8g | Sodium 51mg | Carbs 0g | Fiber 0g | Sugar 0g | Protein 14g

Juicy Paprika Chicken Breast

Servings: 4

Cooking Time: 30 Minutes

Ingredients:

- Oil, for spraying
- 4 (170 g) boneless, skinless chicken breasts
- 1 tablespoon olive oil
- 1 tablespoon paprika
- 1 tablespoon packed light brown sugar
- ½ teaspoon cayenne pepper
- ½ teaspoon onion powder
- ½ teaspoon granulated garlic

Directions:

1. Line the two air fryer drawers with parchment and spray lightly with oil.
2. Brush the chicken with the olive oil.
3. In a small bowl, mix together the paprika, brown sugar, cayenne pepper, onion powder, and garlic and sprinkle it over the chicken.
4. Place the chicken in the two prepared drawers.
5. Air fry at 180°C for 15 minutes, flip, and cook for another 15 minutes, or until the internal temperature reaches 76°C. Serve immediately.

Bang-bang Chicken

Servings: 2

Cooking Time: 20 Minutes

Ingredients:

- 1 cup mayonnaise
- ½ cup sweet chili sauce
- 2 tablespoons Sriracha sauce
- ⅓ cup flour
- 1 lb. boneless chicken breast, diced
- 1 ½ cups panko bread crumbs
- 2 green onions, chopped

Directions:

1. Mix mayonnaise with Sriracha and sweet chili sauce in a large bowl.
2. Keep ¾ cup of the mixture aside.
3. Add flour, chicken, breadcrumbs, and remaining mayo mixture to a resealable plastic bag.
4. Zip the bag and shake well to coat.
5. Divide the chicken in the two crisper plates in a single layer.
6. Return the crisper plate to the Ninja Foodi Dual Zone Air Fryer.
7. Choose the Air Fry mode for Zone 1 and set the temperature to 390 degrees F and the time to 20 minutes|
8. Select the "MATCH" button to copy the settings for Zone 2.
9. Initiate cooking by pressing the START/STOP button.
10. Flip the chicken once cooked halfway through.
11. Top the chicken with reserved mayo sauce.
12. Garnish with green onions and serve warm.

Chicken With Pineapple And Peach

Servings: 4

Cooking Time: 14 To 15 Minutes

Ingredients:

- 1 (450 g) low-sodium boneless, skinless chicken breasts, cut into 1-inch pieces
- 1 medium red onion, chopped
- 1 (230 g) can pineapple chunks, drained, 60 ml juice reserved
- 1 tablespoon peanut oil or safflower oil
- 1 peach, peeled, pitted, and cubed
- 1 tablespoon cornflour
- ½ teaspoon ground ginger
- ¼ teaspoon ground allspice
- Brown rice, cooked (optional)

Directions:

1. Preheat the air fryer to 195°C.
2. In a medium metal bowl, mix the chicken, red onion, pineapple, and peanut oil. Bake in the air fryer for 9 minutes. Remove and stir.
3. Add the peach and return the bowl to the air fryer. Bake for 3 minutes more. Remove and stir again.
4. In a small bowl, whisk the reserved pineapple juice, the cornflour, ginger, and allspice well. Add to the chicken mixture and stir to combine.
5. Bake for 2 to 3 minutes more, or until the chicken reaches an internal temperature of 75°C on a meat thermometer and the sauce is slightly thickened.
6. Serve immediately over hot cooked brown rice, if desired.

Curried Orange Honey Chicken

Servings: 4

Cooking Time: 16 To 19 Minutes

Ingredients:

- 340 g boneless, skinless chicken thighs, cut into 1-inch pieces
- 1 yellow bell pepper, cut into 1½-inch pieces
- 1 small red onion, sliced
- Olive oil for misting
- 60 ml chicken stock
- 2 tablespoons honey
- 60 ml orange juice
- 1 tablespoon cornflour
- 2 to 3 teaspoons curry powder

Directions:

1. Preheat the air fryer to 190°C.
2. Put the chicken thighs, pepper, and red onion in the zone 1 air fryer drawer and mist with olive oil.
3. Roast for 12 to 14 minutes or until the chicken is cooked to 76°C, shaking the drawer halfway through cooking time.
4. Remove the chicken and vegetables from the air fryer drawer and set aside.
5. In a metal bowl, combine the stock, honey, orange juice, cornflour, and curry powder, and mix well. Add the chicken and vegetables, stir, and put the bowl in the drawer.
6. Return the drawer to the air fryer and roast for 2 minutes. Remove and stir, then roast for 2 to 3 minutes or until the sauce is thickened and bubbly.
7. Serve warm.

General Tso's Chicken

Servings: 4
Cooking Time: 22 Minutes

Ingredients:

- 1 egg, large
- ⅓ cup 2 teaspoons cornstarch,
- ¼ teaspoons salt
- ¼ teaspoons ground white pepper
- 7 tablespoons chicken broth
- 2 tablespoons soy sauce
- 2 tablespoons ketchup
- 2 teaspoons sugar
- 2 teaspoons unseasoned rice vinegar
- 1 ½ tablespoons canola oil
- 4 chile de árbol, chopped and seeds discarded
- 1 tablespoon chopped fresh ginger
- 1 tablespoon garlic, chopped
- 2 tablespoons green onion, sliced
- 1 teaspoon toasted sesame oil
- 1 lb. boneless chicken thighs, cut into 1 ¼ -inch chunks
- ½ teaspoon toasted sesame seeds

Directions:

1. Add egg to a large bowl and beat it with a fork.
2. Add chicken to the egg and coat it well.
3. Whisk ⅓ cup of cornstarch with black pepper and salt in a small bowl.
4. Add chicken to the cornstarch mixture and mix well to coat.
5. Divide the chicken in the two crisper plates and spray them cooking oi.
6. Return the crisper plates to the Ninja Foodi Dual Zone Air Fryer.
7. Choose the Air Fry mode for Zone 1 and set the temperature to 390 degrees F and the time to 20 minutes|
8. Select the "MATCH" button to copy the settings for Zone 2.
9. Initiate cooking by pressing the START/STOP button.
10. Once done, remove the air fried chicken from the air fryer.
11. Whisk 2 teaspoons of cornstarch with soy sauce, broth, sugar, ketchup, and rice vinegar in a small bowl.
12. Add chilies and canola oil to a skillet and sauté for 1 minute.
13. Add garlic and ginger, then sauté for 30 seconds.
14. Stir in cornstarch sauce and cook until it bubbles and thickens.
15. Toss in cooked chicken and garnish with sesame oil, sesame seeds, and green onion.
16. Enjoy.

Air Fried Chicken Potatoes With Sun-dried Tomato

Servings: 2
Cooking Time: 25 Minutes

Ingredients:

- 2 teaspoons minced fresh oregano, divided
- 2 teaspoons minced fresh thyme, divided
- 2 teaspoons extra-virgin olive oil, plus extra as needed
- 450 g fingerling potatoes, unpeeled
- 2 (340 g) bone-in split chicken breasts, trimmed
- 1 garlic clove, minced
- 15 g oil-packed sun-dried tomatoes, patted dry and chopped
- 1½ tablespoons red wine vinegar
- 1 tablespoon capers, rinsed and minced
- 1 small shallot, minced
- Salt and ground black pepper, to taste

Directions:

1. Preheat the zone 1 air fryer drawer to 180°C.
2. Combine 1 teaspoon of oregano, 1 teaspoon of thyme, ¼ teaspoon of salt, ¼ teaspoon of ground black pepper, 1 teaspoons of olive oil in a large bowl. Add the potatoes and toss to coat well.
3. Combine the chicken with remaining thyme, oregano, and olive oil. Sprinkle with garlic, salt, and pepper. Toss to coat well.
4. Place the potatoes in the preheated air fryer drawer, then arrange the chicken on top of the potatoes.
5. Air fry for 25 minutes or until the internal temperature of the chicken reaches at least 76°C and the potatoes are wilted. Flip the chicken and potatoes halfway through.
6. Meanwhile, combine the sun-dried tomatoes, vinegar, capers, and shallot in a separate large bowl. Sprinkle with salt and ground black pepper. Toss to mix well.
7. Remove the chicken and potatoes from the air fryer and allow to cool for 10 minutes. Serve with the sun-dried tomato mix.

Chicken Wings With Piri Piri Sauce

Servings: 6

Cooking Time: 30 Minutes

Ingredients:

- 12 chicken wings
- 45 g butter, melted
- 1 teaspoon onion powder
- ½ teaspoon cumin powder
- 1 teaspoon garlic paste
- Sauce:
- 60 g piri piri peppers, stemmed and chopped
- 1 tablespoon pimiento, seeded and minced
- 1 garlic clove, chopped
- 2 tablespoons fresh lemon juice
- ⅓ teaspoon sea salt
- ½ teaspoon tarragon

Directions:

1. Steam the chicken wings using a steamer drawer that is placed over a saucepan with boiling water; reduce the heat.
2. Now, steam the wings for 10 minutes over a moderate heat. Toss the wings with butter, onion powder, cumin powder, and garlic paste.
3. Let the chicken wings cool to room temperature. Then, refrigerate them for 45 to 50 minutes.
4. Roast in the preheated air fryer at 170°C for 25 to 30 minutes; make sure to flip them halfway through.
5. While the chicken wings are cooking, prepare the sauce by mixing all of the sauce ingredients in a food processor. Toss the wings with prepared Piri Piri Sauce and serve.

Spicy Chicken Sandwiches With "fried" Pickles

Servings: 4

Cooking Time: 18 Minutes

Ingredients:

- FOR THE CHICKEN SANDWICHES
- 2 tablespoons all-purpose flour
- 2 large eggs
- 2 teaspoons Louisiana-style hot sauce
- 1 cup panko bread crumbs
- 1 teaspoon paprika
- ½ teaspoon garlic powder
- ¼ teaspoon salt
- ¼ teaspoon freshly ground black pepper
- ¼ teaspoon cayenne pepper (optional)
- 4 thin-sliced chicken cutlets (4 ounces each)
- 2 teaspoons vegetable oil
- 4 hamburger rolls
- FOR THE PICKLES
- 1 cup dill pickle chips, drained
- 1 large egg
- ½ cup panko bread crumbs
- Nonstick cooking spray
- ½ cup ranch dressing, for serving (optional)

Directions:

1. To prep the sandwiches:
2. Set up a breading station with three small shallow bowls. Place the flour in the first bowl. In the second bowl, whisk together the eggs and hot sauce. Combine the panko, paprika, garlic powder, salt, black pepper, and cayenne pepper in the third bowl.
3. Bread the chicken cutlets in this order: First, dip them into the flour, coating both sides. Then, dip into the egg mixture. Finally, coat them in the panko mixture, gently pressing the breading into the chicken to help it adhere. Drizzle the cutlets with the oil.
4. To prep the pickles:
5. Pat the pickles dry with a paper towel.
6. In a small shallow bowl, whisk the egg. Add the panko to a second shallow bowl.
7. Dip the pickles in the egg, then the panko. Mist both sides of the pickles with cooking spray.
8. To cook the chicken and pickles:
9. Install a crisper plate in each of the two baskets. Place the chicken in the Zone 1 basket and insert the basket in the unit. Place the pickles in the Zone 2 basket and insert the basket in the unit.
10. Select Zone 1, select AIR FRY, set the temperature to 390°F, and set the time to 18 minutes.
11. Select Zone 2, select AIR FRY, set the temperature to 400°F, and set the time to 15 minutes. Select SMART FINISH.
12. Press START/PAUSE to begin cooking.
13. When both timers read 10 minutes, press START/PAUSE. Remove the Zone 1 basket and use silicone-tipped tongs to flip the chicken. Reinsert the basket. Remove the Zone 2 basket and shake to redistribute the pickles. Reinsert the basket and press START/PAUSE to resume cooking.
14. When cooking is complete, the breading will be crisp and golden brown and the chicken cooked through . Place one chicken cutlet on each hamburger roll. Serve the "fried" pickles on the side with ranch dressing, if desired.

Chicken Strips With Satay Sauce

Servings: 4

Cooking Time: 10 Minutes

Ingredients:

- 4 (170 g) boneless, skinless chicken breasts, sliced into 16 (1-inch) strips
- 1 teaspoon fine sea salt
- 1 teaspoon paprika
- Sauce:
- 60 g creamy almond butter (or sunflower seed butter for nut-free)
- 2 tablespoons chicken broth
- 1½ tablespoons coconut vinegar or unseasoned rice vinegar
- 1 clove garlic, minced
- 1 teaspoon peeled and minced fresh ginger
- ½ teaspoon hot sauce
- ⅛ teaspoon stevia glycerite, or 2 to 3 drops liquid stevia
- For Garnish/Serving (Optional):
- 15 g chopped coriander leaves
- Red pepper flakes
- Sea salt flakes
- Thinly sliced red, orange, and yellow bell peppers
- Special Equipment:
- 16 wooden or bamboo skewers, soaked in water for 15 minutes

Directions:

1. Spray the zone 1 air fryer drawer with avocado oil. Preheat the air fryer to 200°C. 2. Thread the chicken strips onto the skewers. Season on all sides with the salt and paprika. Place the chicken skewers in the air fryer drawer and air fry for 5 minutes, flip, and cook for another 5 minutes, until the chicken is cooked through and the internal temperature reaches 76°C. 3. While the chicken skewers cook, make the sauce: In a medium-sized bowl, stir together all the sauce ingredients until well combined. Taste and adjust the sweetness and heat to your liking. 4. Garnish the chicken with coriander, red pepper flakes, and salt flakes, if desired, and serve with sliced bell peppers, if desired. Serve the sauce on the side. 5. Store leftovers in an airtight container in the fridge for up to 4 days or in the freezer for up to a month. Reheat in a preheated 180°C air fryer for 3 minutes per side, or until heated through.

Broccoli Cheese Chicken

Servings: 4

Cooking Time: 25 Minutes

Ingredients:

- 1 tablespoon avocado oil
- 15 g chopped onion
- 35 g finely chopped broccoli
- 115 g cream cheese, at room temperature
- 60 g Cheddar cheese, shredded
- 1 teaspoon garlic powder
- ½ teaspoon sea salt, plus additional for seasoning, divided
- ¼ freshly ground black pepper, plus additional for seasoning, divided
- 900 g boneless, skinless chicken breasts
- 1 teaspoon smoked paprika

Directions:

1. Heat a medium skillet over medium-high heat and pour in the avocado oil. Add the onion and broccoli and cook, stirring occasionally, for 5 to 8 minutes, until the onion is tender.
2. Transfer to a large bowl and stir in the cream cheese, Cheddar cheese, and garlic powder, and season to taste with salt and pepper.
3. Hold a sharp knife parallel to the chicken breast and cut a long pocket into one side. Stuff the chicken pockets with the broccoli mixture, using toothpicks to secure the pockets around the filling.
4. In a small dish, combine the paprika, ½ teaspoon salt, and ¼ teaspoon pepper. Sprinkle this over the outside of the chicken.
5. Set the air fryer to 200°C. Place the chicken in a single layer in the two air fryer drawers and cook for 14 to 16 minutes, until an instant-read thermometer reads 70°C. Place the chicken on a plate and tent a piece of aluminum foil over the chicken. Allow to rest for 5 to 10 minutes before serving.

Chicken Breast Strips

Servings:2

Cooking Time:22

Ingredients:

- 2 large organic egg
- 1-ounce buttermilk
- 1 cup of cornmeal
- ¼ cup all-purpose flour
- Salt and black pepper, to taste
- 1 pound of chicken breasts, cut into strips
- 2 tablespoons of oil bay seasoning
- oil spray, for greasing

Directions:

1. Take a medium bowl and whisk eggs with buttermilk.
2. In a separate large bowl mix flour, cornmeal, salt, black pepper, and oil bay seasoning.
3. First, dip the chicken breast strip in egg wash and then dredge into the flour mixture.
4. Coat the strip all over and layer on both the baskets that are already grease with oil spray.
5. Grease the chicken breast strips with oil spray as well.
6. Set the zone 1 basket to AIR FRY mode at 400 degrees F for 22 minutes.
7. Select the MATCH button for zone 2.
8. Hit the start button to let the cooking start.
9. Once the cooking cycle is done, serve.

Nutrition:

- (Per serving) Calories 788| Fat25g| Sodium835 mg | Carbs60g | Fiber 4.9g| Sugar1.5g | Protein79g

Delicious Chicken Skewers

Servings: 4

Cooking Time: 15 Minutes

Ingredients:

- 900g chicken thighs, cut into cubes
- 45ml fresh lime juice
- 59ml coconut milk
- 2 tbsp Thai red curry
- 35ml maple syrup
- 120ml tamari soy sauce

Directions:

1. Add chicken and remaining ingredients into the bowl and mix well.
2. Cover the bowl and place in the refrigerator for 2 hours.
3. Thread the marinated chicken onto the soaked skewers.
4. Insert a crisper plate in the Ninja Foodi air fryer baskets.
5. Place the chicken skewers in both baskets.
6. Select zone 1 then select "air fry" mode and set the temperature to 360 degrees F for 15 minutes. Press "match" to match zone 2 settings to zone 1. Press "start/stop" to begin.

Nutrition:

- (Per serving) Calories 526 | Fat 20.5g |Sodium 2210mg | Carbs 12.9g | Fiber 0.6g | Sugar 10g | Protein 69.7g

Greek Chicken Souvlaki

Servings: 3 To 4

Cooking Time: 15 Minutes

Ingredients:

- Chicken:
- Grated zest and juice of 1 lemon
- 2 tablespoons extra-virgin olive oil
- 1 tablespoon Greek souvlaki seasoning
- 450 g boneless, skinless chicken breast, cut into 2-inch chunks
- Vegetable oil spray
- For Serving:
- Warm pita bread or hot cooked rice
- Sliced ripe tomatoes
- Sliced cucumbers
- Thinly sliced red onion
- Kalamata olives
- Tzatziki

Directions:

1. For the chicken: In a small bowl, combine the lemon zest, lemon juice, olive oil, and souvlaki seasoning. Place the chicken in a gallon-size resealable plastic bag. Pour the marinade over chicken. Seal bag and massage to coat. Place the bag in a large bowl and marinate for 30 minutes, or cover and refrigerate up to 24 hours, turning the bag occasionally. 2. Place the chicken a single layer in the zone 1 air fryer drawer. Cook at 180°C for 10 minutes, turning the chicken and spraying with a little vegetable oil spray halfway through the cooking time. Increase the air fryer temperature to 200°C for 5 minutes to allow the chicken to crisp and brown a little. 3. Transfer the chicken to a serving platter and serve with pita bread or rice, tomatoes, cucumbers, onion, olives and tzatziki.

Jerk Chicken Thighs

Servings: 6
Cooking Time: 15 To 20 Minutes
Ingredients:

- 2 teaspoons ground coriander
- 1 teaspoon ground allspice
- 1 teaspoon cayenne pepper
- 1 teaspoon ground ginger
- 1 teaspoon salt
- 1 teaspoon dried thyme
- ½ teaspoon ground cinnamon
- ½ teaspoon ground nutmeg
- 900 g boneless chicken thighs, skin on
- 2 tablespoons olive oil

Directions:

1. In a small bowl, combine the coriander, allspice, cayenne, ginger, salt, thyme, cinnamon, and nutmeg. Stir until thoroughly combined.
2. Place the chicken in a baking dish and use paper towels to pat dry. Thoroughly coat both sides of the chicken with the spice mixture. Cover and refrigerate for at least 2 hours, preferably overnight.
3. Preheat the air fryer to 180°C.
4. Arrange the chicken in a single layer in the two air fryer drawers and lightly coat with the olive oil. Pausing halfway through the cooking time to flip the chicken, air fry for 15 to 20 minutes, until a thermometer inserted into the thickest part registers 76°C.

Turkey Burger Patties

Servings: 4
Cooking Time: 14 Minutes
Ingredients:

- 1 egg white
- 453g ground turkey
- 30ml Worcestershire sauce
- ½ tsp dried basil
- ½ tsp dried oregano
- Pepper
- Salt

Directions:

1. In a bowl, mix ground turkey with remaining ingredients until well combined.
2. Insert a crisper plate in the Ninja Foodi air fryer baskets.
3. Make patties from the turkey mixture and place them in both baskets.
4. Select zone 1, then select "air fry" mode and set the temperature to 360 degrees F for 14 minutes. Press "match" to match zone 2 settings to zone 1. Press "start/stop" to begin.

Nutrition:

- (Per serving) Calories 234 | Fat 12.5g |Sodium 251mg | Carbs 1.7g | Fiber 0.1g | Sugar 1.6g | Protein 32g

Thai Curry Chicken Kabobs

Servings: 4
Cooking Time: 15 Minutes
Ingredients:

- 900g skinless chicken thighs
- 120ml Tamari
- 60ml coconut milk
- 3 tablespoons lime juice
- 3 tablespoons maple syrup
- 2 tablespoons Thai red curry

Directions:

1. Mix red curry paste, honey, lime juice, coconut milk, soy sauce in a bowl.
2. Add this sauce and chicken to a Ziplock bag.
3. Seal the bag and shake it to coat well.
4. Refrigerate the chicken for 2 hours then thread the chicken over wooden skewers.
5. Divide the skewers in the air fryer baskets.
6. Return the air fryer basket 1 to Zone 1, and basket 2 to Zone 2 of the Ninja Foodi 2-Basket Air Fryer.
7. Choose the "Air Fry" mode for Zone 1 at 350 degrees F and 15 minutes of cooking time.
8. Select the "MATCH COOK" option to copy the settings for Zone 2.
9. Initiate cooking by pressing the START/PAUSE BUTTON.
10. Flip the skewers once cooked halfway through.
11. Serve warm.

Nutrition:

- (Per serving) Calories 353 | Fat 5g |Sodium 818mg | Carbs 53.2g | Fiber 4.4g | Sugar 8g | Protein 17.3g

Bacon-wrapped Chicken

Servings: 2
Cooking Time: 28 Minutes
Ingredients:

- Butter:
- ½ stick butter softened
- ½ garlic clove, minced
- ¼ teaspoon dried thyme
- ¼ teaspoon dried basil
- ⅛ teaspoon coarse salt
- 1 pinch black pepper, ground
- ⅓ lb. thick-cut bacon
- 1 ½ lbs. boneless skinless chicken thighs
- 2 teaspoons garlic, minced

Directions:

1. Mix garlic softened butter with thyme, salt, basil, and black pepper in a bowl.
2. Add butter mixture on a piece of wax paper and roll it up tightly to make a butter log.
3. Place the log in the refrigerator for 2 hours.
4. Spray one bacon strip on a piece of wax paper.
5. Place each chicken thigh on top of one bacon strip and rub it with garlic.
6. Make a slit in the chicken thigh and add a teaspoon of butter to the chicken.
7. Wrap the bacon around the chicken thigh.
8. Repeat those same steps with all the chicken thighs.
9. Place the bacon-wrapped chicken thighs in the two crisper plates.
10. Return the crisper plates to the Ninja Foodi Dual Zone Air Fryer.
11. Choose the Air Fry mode for Zone 1 and set the temperature to 390 degrees F and the time to 28 minutes|
12. Select the "MATCH" button to copy the settings for Zone 2.
13. Initiate cooking by pressing the START/STOP button.
14. Flip the chicken once cooked halfway through, and resume cooking.
15. Serve warm.

Pickled Chicken Fillets

Servings: 4
Cooking Time: 28 Minutes
Ingredients:

- 2 boneless chicken breasts
- ½ cup dill pickle juice
- 2 eggs
- ½ cup milk
- 1 cup flour, all-purpose
- 2 tablespoons powdered sugar
- 2 tablespoons potato starch
- 1 teaspoon paprika
- 1 teaspoon of sea salt
- ½ teaspoon black pepper
- ½ teaspoon garlic powder
- ¼ teaspoon ground celery seed ground
- 1 tablespoon olive oil
- Cooking spray
- 4 hamburger buns, toasted
- 8 dill pickle chips

Directions:

1. Set the chicken in a suitable ziplock bag and pound it into ½ thickness with a mallet.
2. Slice the chicken into 2 halves.
3. Add pickle juice and seal the bag.
4. Refrigerate for 30 minutes approximately for marination. Whisk both eggs with milk in a shallow bowl.
5. Thoroughly mix flour with spices and flour in a separate bowl.
6. Dip each chicken slice in egg, then in the flour mixture.
7. Shake off the excess and set the chicken pieces in the crisper plate.
8. Spray the pieces with cooking oil.
9. Place the chicken pieces in the two crisper plate in a single layer and spray the cooking oil.
10. Return the crisper plate to the Ninja Foodi Dual Zone Air Fryer.
11. Choose the Air Fry mode for Zone 1 and set the temperature to 390 degrees F and the time to 28 minutes|
12. Select the "MATCH" button to copy the settings for Zone 2.
13. Initiate cooking by pressing the START/STOP button.
14. Flip the chicken pieces once cooked halfway through, and resume cooking.
15. Enjoy with pickle chips and a dollop of mayonnaise.

Turkey And Cranberry Quesadillas

Servings: 4
Cooking Time: 4 To 8 Minutes
Ingredients:

- 6 low-sodium whole-wheat tortillas
- 75 g shredded low-sodium low-fat Swiss cheese
- 105 g shredded cooked low-sodium turkey breast
- 2 tablespoons cranberry sauce
- 2 tablespoons dried cranberries
- ½ teaspoon dried basil
- Olive oil spray, for spraying the tortillas

Directions:

1. Preheat the air fryer to 200°C.
2. Put 3 tortillas on a work surface.
3. Evenly divide the Swiss cheese, turkey, cranberry sauce, and dried cranberries among the tortillas. Sprinkle with the basil and top with the remaining tortillas.
4. Spray the outsides of the tortillas with olive oil spray.
5. One at a time, air fry the quesadillas in the air fryer for 4 to 8 minutes, or until crisp and the cheese is melted. Cut into quarters and serve.

Dijon Chicken Wings

Servings: 3
Cooking Time: 20 Minutes
Ingredients:

- 1 cup chicken batter mix, Louisiana
- 9 chicken wings
- ½ teaspoon smoked Paprika
- 2 tablespoons Dijon mustard
- 1 tablespoon cayenne pepper
- 1 teaspoon meat tenderizer, powder
- Oil spray, for greasing

Directions:

1. Pat dry the chicken wings and add mustard, paprika, meat tenderizer, and cayenne pepper.
2. Dredge the wings in the chicken batter mix.
3. Oil spray the chicken wings.
4. Grease both baskets of the air fryer.
5. Divide the wings between the two zones of the air fryer.
6. Set zone 1 to AIR FRY mode at 400 degrees F/ 200 degrees C for 20 minutes.
7. Select MATCH for zone 2.
8. Hit START/STOP button to begin the cooking.
9. Once the cooking cycle is complete, serve, and enjoy hot.

Nutrition:

- (Per serving) Calories 621 | Fat 32.6g | Sodium 2016mg | Carbs 46.6g | Fiber 1.1g | Sugar 0.2g | Protein 32.1g

Thai Chicken Meatballs

Servings: 4
Cooking Time: 10 Minutes
Ingredients:

- ½ cup sweet chili sauce
- 2 tablespoons lime juice
- 2 tablespoons ketchup
- 1 teaspoon soy sauce
- 1 large egg, lightly beaten
- ¾ cup panko breadcrumbs
- 1 green onion, finely chopped
- 1 tablespoon minced fresh cilantro
- ½ teaspoon salt
- ½ teaspoon garlic powder
- 1-pound lean ground chicken

Directions:

1. Combine the chili sauce, lime juice, ketchup, and soy sauce in a small bowl; set aside ½ cup for serving.
2. Combine the egg, breadcrumbs, green onion, cilantro, salt, garlic powder, and the remaining 4 tablespoons chili sauce mixture in a large mixing bowl. Mix in the chicken lightly yet thoroughly. Form into 12 balls.
3. Install a crisper plate in both drawers. Place half the chicken meatballs in the zone 1 drawer and half in zone 2's, then insert the drawers into the unit.
4. Select zone 1, select AIR FRY, set temperature to 390 degrees F/ 200 degrees C, and set time to 10 minutes. Select MATCH to match zone 2 settings to zone 1. Press the START/STOP button to begin cooking.
5. When the time reaches 5 minutes, press START/STOP to pause the unit. Remove the drawers and flip the chicken. Re-insert the drawers into the unit and press START/STOP to resume cooking.
6. When cooking is complete, remove the chicken meatballs and serve hot.

Nutrition:

- (Per serving) Calories 93 | Fat 3g | Sodium 369mg | Carbs 9g | Fiber 0g | Sugar 6g | Protein 9g

Chicken And Broccoli

Servings: 4
Cooking Time: 15 Minutes

Ingredients:

- 1-pound boneless, skinless chicken breast or thighs, cut into 1-inch bite-sized pieces
- ¼ –½ pound broccoli, cut into florets (1–2 cups)
- ½ medium onion, cut into thick slices
- 3 tablespoons olive oil or grape seed oil
- ½ teaspoon garlic powder
- 1 tablespoon fresh minced ginger
- 1 tablespoon low-sodium soy sauce
- 1 tablespoon rice vinegar
- 1 teaspoon sesame oil
- 2 teaspoons hot sauce (optional)
- ½ teaspoon sea salt, or to taste
- Black pepper, to taste
- Lemon wedges, for serving (optional)

Directions:

1. Combine the oil, garlic powder, ginger, soy sauce, rice vinegar, sesame oil, optional spicy sauce, salt, and pepper in a large mixing bowl.
2. Put the chicken in a separate bowl.
3. In a separate bowl, combine the broccoli and onions.
4. Divide the marinade between the two bowls and toss to evenly coat each.
5. Install a crisper plate into both drawers. Place the broccoli in the zone 1 drawer, then insert the drawer into the unit. Place the chicken breasts in the zone 2 drawer, then insert the drawer into the unit.
6. Select zone 1, select AIR FRY, set temperature to 390 degrees F/ 200 degrees C, and set time to 10 minutes. Select zone 2, select AIR FRY, set temperature to 390 degrees F/ 200 degrees C, and set time to 20 minutes. Select SYNC. Press the START/STOP button to begin cooking.
7. When zone 2 time reaches 9 minutes, press START/STOP to pause the unit. Remove the drawer and toss the chicken. Re-insert the drawer into the unit and press START/STOP to resume cooking.
8. When cooking is complete, serve the chicken breasts and broccoli while still hot.
9. Add additional salt and pepper to taste. Squeeze optional fresh lemon juice on top and serve warm.

Nutrition:

- (Per serving) Calories 224 | Fat 15.8g | Sodium 203mg | Carbs 4g | Fiber 1g | Sugar 1g | Protein 25g

Chili Chicken Wings

Servings: 4
Cooking Time: 43 Minutes

Ingredients:

- 8 chicken wings drumettes
- cooking spray
- ⅛ cup low-fat buttermilk
- ¼ cup almond flour
- McCormick Chicken Seasoning to taste
- Thai Chili Marinade
- 1 ½ tablespoons low-sodium soy sauce
- ½ teaspoon ginger, minced
- 1 ½ garlic cloves
- 1 green onion
- ½ teaspoon rice wine vinegar
- ½ tablespoon Sriracha sauce
- ½ tablespoon sesame oil

Directions:

1. Put all the ingredients for the marinade in the blender and blend them for 1 minute.
2. Keep this marinade aside. Pat dry the washed chicken and place it in the Ziploc bag.
3. Add buttermilk, chicken seasoning, and zip the bag.
4. Shake the bag well, then refrigerator for 30 minutes for marination.
5. Remove the chicken drumettes from the marinade, then dredge them through dry flour.
6. Spread the drumettes in the two crisper plate and spray them with cooking oil.
7. Return the crisper plate to the Ninja Foodi Dual Zone Air Fryer.
8. Choose the Air Fry mode for Zone 1 and set the temperature to 390 degrees F and the time to 43 minutes|
9. Select the "MATCH" button to copy the settings for Zone 2.
10. Initiate cooking by pressing the START/STOP button.
11. Toss the drumettes once cooked halfway through.
12. Now brush the chicken pieces with Thai chili sauce and then resume cooking.
13. Serve warm.

Chicken Parmesan With Roasted Lemon-parmesan Broccoli

Servings: 4
Cooking Time: 18 Minutes

Ingredients:

- FOR THE CHICKEN PARMESAN
- 2 tablespoons all-purpose flour
- 2 large eggs
- 1 cup panko bread crumbs
- 2 tablespoons grated Parmesan cheese
- 2 teaspoons Italian seasoning
- 4 thin-sliced chicken cutlets (4 ounces each)
- 2 tablespoons vegetable oil
- ½ cup marinara sauce
- ½ cup shredded part-skim mozzarella cheese
- FOR THE BROCCOLI
- 4 cups broccoli florets
- 2 tablespoons olive oil, divided
- ¼ teaspoon kosher salt
- ¼ teaspoon freshly ground black pepper
- 2 teaspoons fresh lemon juice
- 2 tablespoons grated Parmesan cheese

Directions:

1. To prep the chicken Parmesan:
2. Set up a breading station with 3 small shallow bowls. Place the flour in the first bowl. In the second bowl, beat the eggs. Combine the panko, Parmesan, and Italian seasoning in the third bowl.
3. Bread the chicken cutlets in this order: First, dip them into the flour, coating both sides. Then, dip into the beaten egg. Finally, place in the panko mixture, coating both sides of the cutlets. Drizzle the oil over the cutlets.
4. To prep the broccoli: In a large bowl, combine the broccoli, 1 tablespoon of olive oil, the salt, and black pepper.
5. To cook the chicken and broccoli:
6. Install a crisper plate in the Zone 1 basket. Place the chicken in the basket and insert the basket in the unit. Place the broccoli in the Zone 2 basket and insert the basket in the unit.
7. Select Zone 1, select AIR FRY, set the temperature to 390°F, and set the time to 18 minutes.
8. Select Zone 2, select ROAST, set the temperature to 390°F, and set the time to 15 minutes. Select SMART FINISH.
9. Press START/PAUSE to begin cooking.
10. When the Zone 1 timer reads 10 minutes, press START/PAUSE. Remove the basket and use silicone-tipped tongs to flip the chicken. Reinsert the basket and press START/PAUSE to resume cooking.
11. When the Zone 1 timer reads 2 minutes, press START/PAUSE. Remove the basket and spoon 2 tablespoons of marinara sauce over each chicken cutlet. Sprinkle the mozzarella on top. Reinsert the basket and press START/PAUSE to resume cooking.
12. When cooking is complete, the cheese will be melted and the chicken cooked through . Transfer the broccoli to a large bowl. Add the lemon juice and Parmesan and toss to coat. Serve the chicken and broccoli warm.

Crusted Chicken Breast

Servings: 4
Cooking Time: 28 Minutes

Ingredients:

- 2 large eggs, beaten
- ½ cup all-purpose flour
- 1 ¼ cups panko bread crumbs
- ⅔ cup Parmesan, grated
- 4 teaspoons lemon zest
- 2 teaspoons dried oregano
- Salt, to taste
- 1 teaspoon cayenne pepper
- Freshly black pepper, to taste
- 4 boneless skinless chicken breasts

Directions:

1. Beat eggs in one shallow bowl and spread flour in another shallow bowl.
2. Mix panko with oregano, lemon zest, Parmesan, cayenne, oregano, salt, and black pepper in another shallow bowl.
3. First, coat the chicken with flour first, then dip it in the eggs and coat them with panko mixture.
4. Arrange the prepared chicken in the two crisper plates.
5. Return the crisper plate to the Ninja Foodi Dual Zone Air Fryer.
6. Choose the Air Fry mode for Zone 1 and set the temperature to 390 degrees F and the time to 28 minutes|
7. Select the "MATCH" button to copy the settings for Zone 2.
8. Initiate cooking by pressing the START/STOP button.
9. Flip the half-cooked chicken and continue cooking for 5 minutes until golden.
10. Serve warm.

Pretzel Chicken Cordon Bleu

Servings: 4
Cooking Time: 26 Minutes
Ingredients:

- 5 boneless chicken thighs
- 3 cups pretzels, crushed
- 2 eggs, beaten
- 10 deli honey ham, slices
- 5 Swiss cheese slices
- Cooking spray

Directions:

1. Grind pretzels in a food processor.
2. Pound the chicken tights with a mallet.
3. Top each chicken piece with one cheese slice and 2 ham slices.
4. Roll the chicken pieces and secure with a toothpick.
5. Dip the rolls in the eggs and coat with the breadcrumbs.
6. Place these rolls in the air fryer baskets.
7. Spray them with cooking oil.
8. Return the air fryer basket 1 to Zone 1, and basket 2 to Zone 2 of the Ninja Foodi 2-Basket Air Fryer.
9. Choose the "Air Fry" mode for Zone 1 and set the temperature to 375 degrees F and 26 minutes of cooking time.
10. Select the "MATCH COOK" option to copy the settings for Zone 2.
11. Initiate cooking by pressing the START/PAUSE BUTTON.
12. Flip the rolls once cooked halfway through.
13. Serve warm.

Nutrition:

- (Per serving) Calories 380 | Fat 29g |Sodium 821mg | Carbs 34.6g | Fiber 0g | Sugar 0g | Protein 30g

Stuffed Chicken Florentine

Servings: 4
Cooking Time: 20 Minutes
Ingredients:

- 3 tablespoons pine nuts
- 40 g frozen spinach, thawed and squeezed dry
- 75 g ricotta cheese
- 2 tablespoons grated Parmesan cheese
- 3 cloves garlic, minced
- Salt and freshly ground black pepper, to taste
- 4 small boneless, skinless chicken breast halves (about 680 g)
- 8 slices bacon

Directions:

1. In a large bowl, combine the spinach, ricotta, Parmesan, and garlic. Season to taste with salt and pepper and stir well until thoroughly combined.
2. Using a sharp knife, cut into the chicken breasts, slicing them across and opening them up like a book, but be careful not to cut them all the way through. Sprinkle the chicken with salt and pepper.
3. Spoon equal amounts of the spinach mixture into the chicken, then fold the top of the chicken breast back over the top of the stuffing. Wrap each chicken breast with 2 slices of bacon.
4. Air fry the chicken for 18 to 20 minutes in zone 1 drawer until the bacon is crisp and a thermometer inserted into the thickest part of the chicken registers 76°C.
5. Place the pine nuts in a small pan and set in the zone 2 air fryer drawer. Air fry at 200°C for 2 to 3 minutes until toasted. Remove the pine nuts to a mixing bowl.

Broccoli And Cheese Stuffed Chicken

Servings: 4
Cooking Time: 20 Minutes
Ingredients:

- 60 g cream cheese, softened
- 70 g chopped fresh broccoli, steamed
- 120 g shredded sharp Cheddar cheese
- 4 (170 g) boneless, skinless chicken breasts
- 2 tablespoons mayonnaise
- ¼ teaspoon salt
- ¼ teaspoon garlic powder
- ⅛ teaspoon ground black pepper

Directions:

1. In a medium bowl, combine cream cheese, broccoli, and Cheddar. Cut a 4-inch pocket into each chicken breast. Evenly divide mixture between chicken breasts; stuff the pocket of each chicken breast with the mixture.
2. Spread ¼ tablespoon mayonnaise per side of each chicken breast, then sprinkle both sides of breasts with salt, garlic powder, and pepper.
3. Place stuffed chicken breasts into the two ungreased air fryer drawers so that the open seams face up. Adjust the temperature to 180°C and air fry for 20 minutes, turning chicken halfway through cooking. When done, chicken will be golden and have an internal temperature of at least 76°C. Serve warm.

Yummy Chicken Breasts

Servings:2
Cooking Time:25
Ingredients:

- 4 large chicken breasts, 6 ounces each
- 2 tablespoons of oil bay seasoning
- 1 tablespoon Montreal chicken seasoning
- 1 teaspoon of thyme
- 1/2 teaspoon of paprika
- Salt, to taste
- oil spray, for greasing

Directions:

1. Season the chicken breast pieces with the listed seasoning and let them rest for 40 minutes.
2. Grease both sides of the chicken breast pieces with oil spray.
3. Divide the chicken breast piece between both baskets.
4. Set zone 1 to AIRFRY mode at 400 degrees F, for 15 minutes.
5. Select the MATCH button for another basket.
6. Select pause and take out the baskets and flip the chicken breast pieces, after 15 minutes.
7. Select the zones to 400 degrees F for 10 more minutes using the MATCH cook button.
8. Once it's done serve.

Nutrition:

- (Per serving) Calories 711| Fat 27.7g| Sodium 895mg | Carbs 1.6g | Fiber 0.4g | Sugar 0.1g | Protein 106.3g

Garlic Dill Wings

Servings: 4
Cooking Time: 25 Minutes
Ingredients:

- 900 g bone-in chicken wings, separated at joints
- ½ teaspoon salt
- ½ teaspoon ground black pepper
- ½ teaspoon onion powder
- ½ teaspoon garlic powder
- 1 teaspoon dried dill

Directions:

1. In a large bowl, toss wings with salt, pepper, onion powder, garlic powder, and dill until evenly coated. Place wings into the two ungreased air fryer drawers in a single layer.
2. Adjust the temperature to 200°C and air fry for 25 minutes, shaking the drawer every 7 minutes during cooking. Wings should have an internal temperature of at least 76°C and be golden brown when done. Serve warm.

Spiced Chicken And Vegetables

Servings:1
Cooking Time:45
Ingredients:

- 2 large chicken breasts
- 2 teaspoons of olive oil
- 1 teaspoon of chili powder
- 1 teaspoon of paprika powder
- 1 teaspoon of onion powder
- ½ teaspoon of garlic powder
- 1/4 teaspoon of Cumin
- Salt and black pepper, to taste
- Vegetable Ingredients:
- 2 large potato, cubed
- 4 large carrots cut into bite-size pieces
- 1 tablespoon of olive oil
- Salt and black pepper, to taste

Directions:

1. Take chicken breast pieces and rub olive oil, salt, pepper, chili powder, onion powder, cumin, garlic powder, and paprika.
2. Season the vegetables with olive oil, salt, and black pepper.
3. Now put the chicken breast pieces in the zone 1 basket.
4. Put the vegetables into the zone 2 basket.
5. Now hit 1 for the first basket and set it to ROAST at 350 degrees F, for 45 minutes.
6. For the second basket hit 2 and set time for 45 minutes, by selecting AIR FRY mode at 350 degrees F.
7. To start cooking hit the smart finish button and press hit start.
8. Once the cooking cycle is done, serve, and enjoy.

Nutrition:

- (Per serving) Calories1510 | Fat 51.3g| Sodium 525mg | Carbs 163g | Fiber24.7 g | Sugar 21.4g | Protein 102.9

Chicken Tenders And Curly Fries

Servings: 4
Cooking Time: 35 Minutes

Ingredients:

- 1-pound frozen chicken tenders
- 1-pound frozen curly French fries
- Dipping sauces of your choice

Directions:

1. Place a crisper plate in each drawer. In the zone 1 drawer, place the chicken tenders, then place the drawer into the unit.
2. Fill the zone 2 drawer with the curly French fries, then place the drawer in the unit.
3. Select zone 1, then AIR FRY, and set the temperature to 390 degrees F/ 200 degrees C with a 22-minute timer. Select zone 2, then AIR FRY, and set the temperature to 400 degrees F/ 200 degrees C with a 30-minute timer. Select SYNC. To begin cooking, press the START/STOP button.
4. Press START/STOP to pause the device when the zone 1 and 2 times reach 8 minutes. Shake the drawers for 10 seconds after removing them from the unit. To resume cooking, re-insert the drawers into the unit and press START/STOP.
5. Enjoy!

Nutrition:

- (Per serving) Calories 500 | Fat 19.8g | Sodium 680mg | Carbs 50.1g | Fiber 4.1g | Sugar 0g | Protein 27.9g

Wings With Corn On Cob

Servings:2
Cooking Time:40

Ingredients:

- 6 chicken wings, skinless
- 2 tablespoons of coconut amino
- 2 tablespoons of brown sugar
- 1 teaspoon of ginger, paste
- ½ inch garlic, minced
- Salt and black pepper to taste
- 2 corn on cobs, small
- Oil spray, for greasing

Directions:

1. Spay the corns with oil spray and season them with salt.
2. Rub the ingredients well.
3. Coat the chicken wings with coconut amino, brown sugar, ginger, garlic, salt, and black pepper.
4. Spray the wings with a good amount of oil spray.
5. Now put the chicken wings in the zone 1 basket.
6. Put the corn into the zone 2 basket.
7. Select ROAST function for chicken wings, press 1, and set time to 23 minutes at 400 degrees F.
8. Press 2 and select the AIR FRY function for corn and set the timer to 40 at 300 degrees F.
9. Once it's done, serve and enjoy.

Nutrition:

- (Per serving) Calories 950| Fat33.4g | Sodium592 mg | Carbs27. 4g | Fiber2.1g | Sugar11.3 g | Protein129 g

Herbed Turkey Breast With Simple Dijon Sauce

Servings: 4
Cooking Time: 30 Minutes

Ingredients:

- 1 teaspoon chopped fresh sage
- 1 teaspoon chopped fresh tarragon
- 1 teaspoon chopped fresh thyme leaves
- 1 teaspoon chopped fresh rosemary leaves
- 1½ teaspoons sea salt
- 1 teaspoon ground black pepper
- 1 (900 g) turkey breast
- 3 tablespoons Dijon mustard
- 3 tablespoons butter, melted
- Cooking spray

Directions:

1. Preheat the air fryer to 200°C. Spritz the two air fryer drawers with cooking spray.
2. Combine the herbs, salt, and black pepper in a small bowl. Stir to mix well. Set aside.
3. Combine the Dijon mustard and butter in a separate bowl. Stir to mix well.
4. Rub the turkey with the herb mixture on a clean work surface, then brush the turkey with Dijon mixture.
5. Arrange the turkey in the two preheated air fryer drawers. Air fry for 30 minutes or until an instant-read thermometer inserted in the thickest part of the turkey breast reaches at least 76°C.
6. Transfer the cooked turkey breast on a large plate and slice to serve.

Chicken Legs With Leeks

Servings: 6
Cooking Time: 18 Minutes

Ingredients:

- 2 leeks, sliced
- 2 large-sized tomatoes, chopped
- 3 cloves garlic, minced
- ½ teaspoon dried oregano
- 6 chicken legs, boneless and skinless
- ½ teaspoon smoked cayenne pepper
- 2 tablespoons olive oil
- A freshly ground nutmeg

Directions:

1. In a mixing dish, thoroughly combine all ingredients, minus the leeks. Place in the refrigerator and let it marinate overnight.
2. Lay the leeks onto the bottom of the two air fryer drawers. Top with the chicken legs.
3. Roast chicken legs at 190°C for 18 minutes, turning halfway through. Serve with hoisin sauce.

Desserts Recipes

Double Chocolate Brownies

Servings: 8
Cooking Time: 15 To 20 Minutes

Ingredients:

- 110 g almond flour
- 50 g unsweetened cocoa powder
- ½ teaspoon baking powder
- 35 g powdered sweetener
- ¼ teaspoon salt
- 110 g unsalted butter, melted and cooled
- 3 eggs
- 1 teaspoon vanilla extract
- 2 tablespoons mini semisweet chocolate chips

Directions:

1. Preheat the air fryer to 175°C. Line a cake pan with baking paper and brush with oil.
2. In a large bowl, combine the almond flour, cocoa powder, baking powder, sweetener, and salt. Add the butter, eggs, and vanilla. Stir until thoroughly combined Spread the batter into the prepared pan and scatter the chocolate chips on top.
3. Air fry in the zone 1 basket for 15 to 20 minutes until the edges are set Let cool completely before slicing. To store, cover and refrigerate the brownies for up to 3 days.

Pumpkin Muffins With Cinnamon

Servings: 4
Cooking Time: 20 Minutes

Ingredients:

- 1 and ½ cups all-purpose flour
- ½ teaspoon baking soda
- ½ teaspoon baking powder
- 1 and ¼ teaspoons cinnamon, groaned
- ¼ teaspoon ground nutmeg, grated
- 2 large eggs
- Salt, pinch
- ¾ cup granulated sugar
- ½ cup dark brown sugar
- 1 and ½ cups pumpkin puree
- ¼ cup coconut milk

Directions:

1. Take 4 ramekins and layer them with muffin paper.
2. In a bowl, add the eggs, brown sugar, baking soda, baking powder, cinnamon, nutmeg, and sugar and whisk well with an electric mixer.
3. In a second bowl, mix the flour, and salt.
4. Slowly add the dry to the wet Ingredients:.
5. Fold in the pumpkin puree and milk and mix it in well.
6. Divide this batter into 4 ramekins.
7. Place two ramekins in each air fryer basket.
8. Set the time for zone 1 to 18 minutes at 360 degrees on AIR FRY mode.
9. Select the MATCH button for the zone 2 basket.
10. Check after the time is up and if not done, and let it AIR FRY for one more minute.
11. Once it is done, serve.

Zesty Cranberry Scones

Servings: 8

Cooking Time: 16 Minutes.

Ingredients:

- 4 cups of flour
- ½ cup brown sugar
- 2 tablespoons baking powder
- ½ teaspoon ground nutmeg
- ½ teaspoon salt
- ½ cup butter, chilled and diced
- 2 cups fresh cranberry
- ⅔ cup sugar
- 2 tablespoons orange zest
- 1 ¼ cups half and half cream
- 2 eggs

Directions:

1. Whisk flour with baking powder, salt, nutmeg, and both the sugars in a bowl.
2. Stir in egg and cream, mix well to form a smooth dough.
3. Fold in cranberries along with the orange zest.
4. Knead this dough well on a work surface.
5. Cut 3-inch circles out of the dough.
6. Divide the scones in the crisper plates and spray them with cooking oil.
7. Return the crisper plates to the Ninja Foodi Dual Zone Air Fryer.
8. Choose the Air Fry mode for Zone 1 and set the temperature to 375 degrees F and the time to 16 minutes.
9. Select the "MATCH" button to copy the settings for Zone 2.
10. Initiate cooking by pressing the START/STOP button.
11. Flip the scones once cooked halfway and resume cooking.
12. Enjoy!

Nutrition:

- (Per serving) Calories 204 | Fat 9g |Sodium 91mg | Carbs 27g | Fiber 2.4g | Sugar 15g | Protein 1.3g

Victoria Sponge Cake

Servings: 8

Cooking Time: 16 Minutes

Ingredients:

- Sponge Cake Ingredients
- 400g self-rising flour
- 450g caster sugar
- 50g lemon curd
- 200g butter
- 4 medium eggs
- 1 tablespoon vanilla essence
- 480ml skimmed milk
- 1 tablespoon olive oil
- 4 tablespoons strawberry jam
- Strawberry buttercream
- 115g butter
- 210g icing sugar
- ½ teaspoon strawberry food coloring
- 1 tablespoon single cream
- 1 teaspoon vanilla essence
- 1 teaspoon maple syrup

Directions:

1. Mix sugar and butter in a bowl using a hand mixer.
2. Beat eggs with oil, and vanilla in a bowl with the mixer until creamy.
3. Stir in milk, flour and curd then mix well.
4. Add butter mixture then mix well.
5. Divide this mixture in two 4 inches greased cake pans.
6. Place one pan in each air fryer basket.
7. Return the air fryer basket 1 to Zone 1, and basket 2 to Zone 2 of the Ninja Foodi 2-Basket Air Fryer.
8. Choose the "Air Fry" mode for Zone 1 and set the temperature to 375 degrees F and 16 minutes of cooking time.
9. Select the "MATCH COOK" option to copy the settings for Zone 2.
10. Initiate cooking by pressing the START/PAUSE BUTTON.
11. Meanwhile, blend the buttercream ingredients in a mixer until fluffy.
12. Place one cake on a plate and top it with the buttercream.
13. Top it jam and then with the other cake.
14. Serve.

Nutrition:

- (Per serving) Calories 284 | Fat 16g |Sodium 252mg | Carbs 31.6g | Fiber 0.9g | Sugar 6.6g | Protein 3.7g

Moist Chocolate Espresso Muffins

Servings: 8
Cooking Time: 18 Minutes

Ingredients:

- 1 egg
- 177ml milk
- ½ tsp baking soda
- ½ tsp espresso powder
- ½ tsp baking powder
- 50g cocoa powder
- 78ml vegetable oil
- 1 tsp apple cider vinegar
- 1 tsp vanilla
- 150g brown sugar
- 150g all-purpose flour
- ½ tsp salt

Directions:

1. In a bowl, whisk egg, vinegar, oil, brown sugar, vanilla, and milk.
2. Add flour, cocoa powder, baking soda, baking powder, espresso powder, and salt and stir until well combined.
3. Pour batter into the silicone muffin moulds.
4. Insert a crisper plate in Ninja Foodi air fryer baskets.
5. Place muffin moulds in both baskets.
6. Select zone 1 then select "bake" mode and set the temperature to 320 degrees F for 18 minutes. Press match cook to match zone 2 settings to zone 1. Press "start/stop" to begin.

Nutrition:

- (Per serving) Calories 222 | Fat 11g |Sodium 251mg | Carbs 29.6g | Fiber 2g | Sugar 14.5g | Protein 4g

Cinnamon Sugar Dessert Fries

Servings: 4
Cooking Time: 15 Minutes

Ingredients:

- 2 sweet potatoes
- 1 tablespoon butter, melted
- 1 teaspoon butter, melted
- 2 tablespoons sugar
- ½ teaspoon ground cinnamon

Directions:

1. Peel and cut the sweet potatoes into skinny fries.
2. Coat the fries with 1 tablespoon of butter.
3. Install a crisper plate into each drawer. Place half the sweet potatoes in the zone 1 drawer and half in zone 2's, then insert the drawers into the unit.
4. Select zone 1, select AIR FRY, set temperature to 390°F, and set time to 15 minutes. Select MATCH to match zone 2 settings to zone 1. Press the START/STOP button to begin cooking.
5. When the time reaches 11 minutes, press START/STOP to pause the unit. Remove the drawers and flip the fries. Re-insert the drawers into the unit and press START/STOP to resume cooking.
6. Meanwhile, mix the 1 teaspoon of butter, the sugar, and the cinnamon in a large bowl.
7. When the fries are done, add them to the bowl, and toss them to coat.
8. Serve and enjoy!

Sweet Protein Powder Doughnut Holes

Servings: 6 (2 Per Serving)
Cooking Time: 6 Minutes

Ingredients:

- ½ cup blanched finely ground almond flour
- ½ cup low-carb vanilla protein powder
- ½ cup granular erythritol
- ½ teaspoon baking powder
- 1 large egg
- 5 tablespoons unsalted butter, melted
- ½ teaspoon vanilla extract

Directions:

1. Stir all ingredients well in a large bowl. Put into the freezer for at least 20 minutes.
2. Wet your hands with water, then form the dough into 12 balls with your hands.
3. Slice a sheet of parchment which fit your air fryer basket. Handling in batches if needed, put doughnut holes into the air fryer basket onto the parchment.
4. Set the temperature to 380°F, then set the timer for 6 minutes.
5. Turn doughnut holes over halfway through the cooking time.
6. Allow them to cool fully before serving.

Coconut Muffins And Dark Chocolate Lava Cake

Servings: 9
Cooking Time: 25 Minutes

Ingredients:

- Coconut Muffins:
- 55 g coconut flour
- 2 tablespoons cocoa powder
- 3 tablespoons granulated sweetener
- 1 teaspoon baking powder
- 2 tablespoons coconut oil
- 2 eggs, beaten
- 50 g desiccated coconut
- Dark Chocolate Lava Cake:
- Olive oil cooking spray
- 30 g whole wheat flour
- 1 tablespoon unsweetened dark chocolate cocoa powder
- 1/8 teaspoon salt
- 1/2 teaspoon baking powder
- 60 ml raw honey
- 1 egg
- 2 tablespoons olive oil

Directions:

1. Make the Coconut Muffins :
2. In the mixing bowl, mix all ingredients.
3. Then pour the mixture into the molds of the muffin and transfer in the zone 1 air fryer basket.
4. Cook the muffins at 175°C for 25 minutes.
5. Make the Dark Chocolate Lava Cake :
6. Preheat the air fryer to 190°C. Lightly coat the insides of four ramekins with olive oil cooking spray.
7. In a medium bowl, combine the flour, cocoa powder, salt, baking powder, honey, egg, and olive oil.
8. Divide the batter evenly among the ramekins.
9. Place the filled ramekins inside the zone 2 air fryer basket and bake for 10 minutes.
10. Remove the lava cakes from the air fryer and slide a knife around the outside edge of each cake. Turn each ramekin upside down on a saucer and serve.

Air Fried Bananas

Servings: 4
Cooking Time: 15 Minutes

Ingredients:

- 4 bananas, sliced
- 1 avocado oil cooking spray

Directions:

1. Spread the banana slices in the two crisper plates in a single layer.
2. Drizzle avocado oil over the banana slices.
3. Return the crisper plate to the Ninja Foodi Dual Zone Air Fryer.
4. Choose the Air Fry mode for Zone 1 and set the temperature to 350 degrees F and the time to 13 minutes.
5. Select the "MATCH" button to copy the settings for Zone 2.
6. Initiate cooking by pressing the START/STOP button.
7. Serve.

Citrus Mousse

Servings: 4
Cooking Time: 12 Minutes

Ingredients:

- 8 ounces cream cheese, softened
- 1 cup heavy cream
- 4 tablespoons fresh lime juice
- 4 tablespoons maple syrup
- Pinch of salt

Directions:

1. For mousse: Press "Zone 1" and "Zone 2" and then rotate the knob for each zone to select "Bake".
2. Set the temperature to 350 degrees F/ 175 degrees C for both zones and then set the time for 5 minutes to preheat.
3. In a bowl, add all the ingredients and mix until well combined.
4. Transfer the mixture into 4 ramekins.
5. After preheating, arrange 2 ramekins into the basket of each zone.
6. Slide each basket into Air Fryer and set the time for 12 minutes.
7. After cooking time is completed, remove the ramekins from Air Fryer.
8. Set the ramekins aside to cool.
9. Refrigerate the ramekins for at least 3 hours before serving.

Molten Chocolate Almond Cakes

Servings: 3
Cooking Time: 13 Minutes
Ingredients:

- Butter and flour for the ramekins
- 110 g bittersweet chocolate, chopped
- 110 gunsalted butter
- 2 eggs
- 2 egg yolks
- 50 g granulated sugar
- ½ teaspoon pure vanilla extract, or almond extract
- 1 tablespoon plain flour
- 3 tablespoons ground almonds
- 8 to 12 semisweet chocolate discs (or 4 chunks of chocolate)
- Cocoa powder or icing sugar, for dusting
- Toasted almonds, coarsely chopped

Directions:

1. Butter and flour three ramekins.
2. Melt the chocolate and butter together, either in the microwave or in a double boiler. In a separate bowl, beat the eggs, egg yolks and sugar together until light and smooth. Add the vanilla extract. Whisk the chocolate mixture into the egg mixture. Stir in the flour and ground almonds.
3. Preheat the air fryer to 165°C.
4. Transfer the batter carefully to the buttered ramekins, filling halfway. Place two or three chocolate discs in the center of the batter and then fill the ramekins to ½-inch below the top with the remaining batter. Place the ramekins into the zone 1 air fryer basket and air fry for 13 minutes. The sides of the cake should be set, but the centers should be slightly soft. Remove the ramekins from the air fryer and let the cakes sit for 5 minutes.
5. Run a butter knife around the edge of the ramekins and invert the cakes onto a plate. Lift the ramekin off the plate slowly and carefully so that the cake doesn't break. Dust with cocoa powder or icing sugar and serve with a scoop of ice cream and some coarsely chopped toasted almonds.

Stuffed Apples

Servings: 8
Cooking Time: 10 Minutes
Ingredients:

- 8 small firm apples, cored
- 1 cup golden raisins
- 1 cup blanched almonds
- 4 tablespoons sugar
- ¼ teaspoon ground cinnamon

Directions:

1. In a food processor, add raisins, almonds, sugar and cinnamon and pulse until chopped.
2. Carefully stuff each apple with raisin mixture.
3. Line each basket of "Zone 1" and "Zone 2" with parchment paper.
4. Press "Zone 1" and "Zone 2" and then rotate the knob for each zone to select "Air Fry".
5. Set the temperature to 355 degrees F/ 180 degrees C for both zones and then set the time for 5 minutes to preheat.
6. After preheating, arrange 4 apples into the basket of each zone.
7. Slide each basket into Air Fryer and set the time for 10 minutes.
8. After cooking time is completed, remove the apples from Air Fryer.
9. Transfer the apples onto plates and set aside to cool slightly before serving.

Chocolate Pudding

Servings: 2
Cooking Time: 12 Minutes
Ingredients:

- 1 egg
- 32g all-purpose flour
- 35g cocoa powder
- 50g sugar
- 57g butter, melted
- ½ tsp baking powder

Directions:

1. In a bowl, mix flour, cocoa powder, sugar, and baking powder.
2. Add egg and butter and stir until well combined.
3. Pour batter into the two greased ramekins.
4. Insert a crisper plate in Ninja Foodi air fryer baskets.
5. Place ramekins in both baskets.
6. Select zone 1 then select "bake" mode and set the temperature to 375 degrees F for 12 minutes. Press match cook to match zone 2 settings to zone 1. Press "start/stop" to begin.

Nutrition:

- (Per serving) Calories 512 | Fat 27.3g |Sodium 198mg | Carbs 70.6g | Fiber 4.7g | Sugar 50.5g | Protein 7.2g

Spiced Apple Cake

Servings: 6
Cooking Time: 30 Minutes

Ingredients:

- Vegetable oil
- 2 diced & peeled Gala apples
- 1 tablespoon fresh lemon juice
- 55 g unsalted butter, softened
- 65 g granulated sugar
- 2 large eggs
- 155 g plain flour
- 1½ teaspoons baking powder
- 1 tablespoon apple pie spice
- ½ teaspoon ground ginger
- ¼ teaspoon ground cardamom
- ¼ teaspoon ground nutmeg
- ½ teaspoon kosher, or coarse sea salt
- 60 ml whole milk
- Icing sugar, for dusting

Directions:

1. Grease a 0.7-liter Bundt, or tube pan with oil; set aside.
2. In a medium bowl, toss the apples with the lemon juice until well coated; set aside.
3. In a large bowl, combine the butter and sugar. Beat with an electric hand mixer on medium speed until the sugar has dissolved. Add the eggs and beat until fluffy. Add the flour, baking powder, apple pie spice, ginger, cardamom, nutmeg, salt, and milk. Mix until the batter is thick but pourable.
4. Pour the batter into the prepared pan. Top batter evenly with the apple mixture. Place the pan in the zone 1 air fryer drawer. Set the temperature to 176°C and cook for 30 minutes, or until a toothpick inserted in the center of the cake comes out clean. Close the air fryer and let the cake rest for 10 minutes. Turn the cake out onto a wire rack and cool completely.
5. Right before serving, dust the cake with icing sugar.

Chocolate Cookies

Servings: 18
Cooking Time: 7 Minutes

Ingredients:

- 96g flour
- 57g butter, softened
- 15ml milk
- 7.5g cocoa powder
- 80g chocolate chips
- ½ tsp vanilla
- 35g sugar
- ¼ tsp baking soda
- Pinch of salt

Directions:

1. In a bowl, mix flour, cocoa powder, sugar, baking soda, vanilla, butter, milk, and salt until well combined.
2. Add chocolate chips and mix well.
3. Insert a crisper plate in Ninja Foodi air fryer baskets.
4. Make cookies from the mixture and place in both baskets.
5. Select zone 1 then select "air fry" mode and set the temperature to 360 degrees F for 7 minutes. Press "match" to match zone 2 settings to zone 1. Press "start/stop" to begin.

Nutrition:

- (Per serving) Calories 82 | Fat 4.1g |Sodium 47mg | Carbs 10.7g | Fiber 0.4g | Sugar 6.2g | Protein 1g

Butter Cake

Servings: 6
Cooking Time: 20 Minutes

Ingredients:

- 1 egg
- 3 tablespoons butter, softened
- ½ cup milk
- 1 tablespoon icing sugar
- ½ cup caster sugar
- 1½ cup plain flour
- A pinch of salt

Directions:

1. In a bowl, add the butter and sugar. Whisk until creamy.
2. Now, add the egg and whisk until fluffy.
3. Add the flour and salt. Mix well with the milk.
4. Place the mixture evenly into the greased cake pan.
5. Press "Zone 1" and "Zone 2" and then rotate the knob for each zone to select "Air Fry".
6. Set the temperature to 350 degrees F/ 175 degrees C for both zones and then set the time for 5 minutes to preheat.
7. After preheating, arrange the pan into the basket of each zone.
8. Slide each basket into Air Fryer and set the time for 15 minutes.
9. After cooking time is completed, remove the pan from Air Fryer.
10. Set aside to cool.
11. Serve and enjoy!

S'mores Dip With Cinnamon-sugar Tortillas

Servings:4
Cooking Time: 5 Minutes
Ingredients:

- FOR THE S'MORES DIP
- ½ cup chocolate-hazelnut spread
- ¼ cup milk chocolate or white chocolate chips
- ¼ cup graham cracker crumbs
- ½ cup mini marshmallows
- FOR THE CINNAMON-SUGAR TORTILLAS
- 4 (6-inch) flour tortillas
- Butter-flavored cooking spray
- 1 teaspoon granulated sugar
- ½ teaspoon ground cinnamon
- ¼ teaspoon ground cardamom (optional)

Directions:

1. To prep the s'mores dip: Spread the chocolate-hazelnut spread in the bottom of a shallow ovenproof ramekin or dish.
2. Scatter the chocolate chips and graham cracker crumbs over the top. Arrange the marshmallows in a single layer on top of the crumbs.
3. To prep the tortillas: Spray both sides of each tortilla with cooking spray. Cut each tortilla into 8 wedges and sprinkle both sides evenly with sugar, cinnamon, and cardamom (if using).
4. To cook the dip and tortillas: Install a crisper plate in each of the two baskets. Place the ramekin in the Zone 1 basket and insert the basket in the unit. Place the tortillas in the Zone 2 basket and insert the basket in the unit.
5. Select Zone 1, select BAKE, set the temperature to 330°F, and set the timer to 5 minutes.
6. Select Zone 2, select AIR FRY, set the temperature to 375°F, and set the timer to 5 minutes. Select SMART FINISH.
7. Press START/PAUSE to begin cooking.
8. When the Zone 2 timer reads 3 minutes, press START/PAUSE. Remove the basket and shake it to redistribute the chips. Reinsert the basket and press START/PAUSE to resume cooking.
9. When cooking is complete, the dip will be bubbling and golden brown and the chips crispy.
10. If desired, toast the marshmallows more: Select Zone 1, select AIR BROIL, set the temperature to 450°F, and set the timer to 1 minute. Cook until the marshmallows are deep golden brown.
11. Let the dip cool for 2 to 3 minutes. Serve with the cinnamon-sugar tortilla chips.

Nutrition:

- (Per serving) Calories: 404; Total fat: 18g; Saturated fat: 7g; Carbohydrates: 54g; Fiber: 2.5g; Protein: 6g; Sodium: 346mg

Easy Mini Chocolate Chip Pan Cookie

Servings: 4
Cooking Time: 7 Minutes
Ingredients:

- ½ cup blanched finely ground almond flour
- ¼ cup powdered erythritol
- 2 tablespoons unsalted butter, softened
- 1 large egg
- ½ teaspoon unflavored gelatin
- ½ teaspoon baking powder
- ½ teaspoon vanilla extract
- 2 tablespoons low-carb, sugar-free chocolate chips

Directions:

1. Combine erythritol and almond flour in a large bowl. Add in egg, gelatin, and butter , stir well.
2. Stir in vanilla and baking powder and then fold in chocolate chips. Spoon batter into 6&quot| round baking pan. Put pan into the air fryer basket.
3. Set the temperature to 300°F, then set the timer for 7 minutes.
4. The top of the cookie will be golden brown and a toothpick inserted in center will come out clean when fully cooked. Allow to rest for more than 10 minutes.

Quickie Cinnamon Sugar Pork Rinds

Servings: 2
Cooking Time: 5 Minutes
Ingredients:

- 2 ounces pork rinds
- 2 tablespoons unsalted butter, melted
- ½ teaspoon ground cinnamon
- ¼ cup powdered erythritol

Directions:

1. Stir butter and pork rinds in a large bowl. Sprinkle with erythritol and cinnamon, then toss to coat well.
2. Put pork rinds into the air fryer basket.
3. Set the temperature to 400°F, then set the timer for 5 minutes.
4. Serve warm.

Cinnamon Bread Twists

Servings: 4
Cooking Time: 15 Minutes

Ingredients:

- Bread Twists Dough
- 120g all-purpose flour
- 1 teaspoon baking powder
- ¼ teaspoon salt
- 150g fat free Greek yogurt
- Brushing
- 2 tablespoons light butter
- 2 tablespoons granulated sugar
- 1-2 teaspoons ground cinnamon, to taste

Directions:

1. Mix flour, salt and baking powder in a bowl.
2. Stir in yogurt and the rest of the dough ingredients in a bowl.
3. Mix well and make 8 inches long strips out of this dough.
4. Twist the strips and place them in the air fryer baskets.
5. Return the air fryer basket 1 to Zone 1, and basket 2 to Zone 2 of the Ninja Foodi 2-Basket Air Fryer.
6. Choose the "Air Fry" mode for Zone 1 at 375 degrees F and 15 minutes of cooking time.
7. Select the "MATCH COOK" option to copy the settings for Zone 2.
8. Initiate cooking by pressing the START/PAUSE BUTTON.
9. Flip the twists once cooked halfway through.
10. Mix butter with cinnamon and sugar in a bowl.
11. Brush this mixture over the twists.
12. Serve.

Nutrition:

- (Per serving) Calories 391 | Fat 24g |Sodium 142mg | Carbs 38.5g | Fiber 3.5g | Sugar 21g | Protein 6.6g

Mocha Pudding Cake Vanilla Pudding Cake

Servings:8
Cooking Time: 25 Minutes

Ingredients:

- FOR THE MOCHA PUDDING CAKE
- 1 cup all-purpose flour
- ⅔ cup granulated sugar
- 1 cup packed light brown sugar, divided
- 5 tablespoons unsweetened cocoa powder, divided
- 2 teaspoons baking powder
- ¼ teaspoon kosher salt
- ½ cup unsweetened almond milk
- 2 teaspoons vanilla extract
- 2 tablespoons vegetable oil
- 1 cup freshly brewed coffee
- FOR THE VANILLA PUDDING CAKE
- 1 cup all-purpose flour
- ⅔ cup granulated sugar, plus ½ cup
- 2 teaspoons baking powder
- ¼ teaspoon kosher salt
- ½ cup unsweetened almond milk
- 2½ teaspoons vanilla extract, divided
- 2 tablespoons vegetable oil
- ¾ cup hot water
- 2 teaspoons cornstarch

Directions:

1. To prep the mocha pudding cake: In a medium bowl, combine the flour, granulated sugar, ½ cup of brown sugar, 3 tablespoons of cocoa powder, the baking powder, and salt. Stir in the almond milk, vanilla, and oil to form a thick batter.
2. Spread the batter in the bottom of the Zone 1 basket. Sprinkle the remaining ½ cup brown sugar and 2 tablespoons of cocoa powder in an even layer over the batter. Gently pour the hot coffee over the batter (do not mix).
3. To prep the vanilla pudding cake: In a medium bowl, combine the flour, ⅔ cup of granulated sugar, the baking powder, and salt. Stir in the almond milk, 2 teaspoons of vanilla, and the oil to form a thick batter.
4. Spread the batter in the bottom of the Zone 2 basket.
5. In a small bowl, whisk together the hot water, cornstarch, and remaining ½ cup of sugar and ½ teaspoon of vanilla. Gently pour over the batter (do not mix).
6. To cook both pudding cakes: Insert both baskets in the unit.
7. Select Zone 1, select BAKE, set the temperature to 330°F, and set the timer to 25 minutes. Select MATCH COOK to match Zone 2 settings to Zone 1.
8. Press START/PAUSE to begin cooking.
9. When cooking is complete, the tops of the cakes should be dry and set.
10. Let the cakes rest for 10 minutes before serving. The pudding will thicken as it cools.

Nutrition:

- (Per serving) Calories: 531; Total fat: 8g; Saturated fat: 1g; Carbohydrates: 115g; Fiber: 3.5g; Protein: 5g; Sodium: 111mg

Pumpkin Muffins

Servings:4
Cooking Time:20

Ingredients:

- 1 and ½ cups of all-purpose flour
- ½ teaspoon baking soda
- ½ teaspoon of baking powder
- 1 and 1/4 teaspoons cinnamon, groaned
- 1/4 teaspoon ground nutmeg, grated
- 2 large eggs
- Salt, pinch
- 3/4 cup granulated sugar
- 1/2 cup dark brown sugar
- 1 and 1/2 cups of pumpkin puree
- 1/4 cup coconut milk

Directions:

1. Take 4 ramekins that are the size of a cup and layer them with muffin papers.
2. Crack an egg in a bowl and add brown sugar, baking soda, baking powder, cinnamon, nutmeg, and sugar.
3. Whisk it all very well with an electric hand beater.
4. Now, in a second bowl, mix the flour, and salt.
5. Now, mix the dry ingredients slowly with the wet ingredients.
6. Now, at the end fold in the pumpkin puree and milk, mix it well
7. Divide this batter into 4 ramekins.
8. Now, divide ramekins between both zones.
9. Set the time for zone 1 to 18 minutes at 360 degrees Fat AIRFRY mode.
10. Select the MATCH button for the zone 2 basket.
11. Check if not done, and let it AIR FRY for one more minute.
12. Once it is done, serve.

Nutrition:

- (Per serving) Calories 291| Fat6.4 g| Sodium 241mg | Carbs 57.1g | Fiber 4.4g | Sugar42 g | Protein 5.9g

Apple Crumble Peach Crumble

Servings:8
Cooking Time: 20 Minutes

Ingredients:

- FOR THE APPLE CRUMBLE
- ½ cup packed light brown sugar
- ¼ cup all-purpose flour
- ¼ cup rolled oats
- 2 tablespoons unsalted butter, at room temperature
- ½ teaspoon ground cinnamon
- ¼ teaspoon ground nutmeg
- ⅛ teaspoon kosher salt
- 4 medium Granny Smith apples, sliced
- FOR THE PEACH CRUMBLE
- ½ cup packed light brown sugar
- ¼ cup all-purpose flour
- ¼ cup rolled oats
- 2 tablespoons unsalted butter, at room temperature
- ½ teaspoon ground cinnamon
- ⅛ teaspoon kosher salt
- 4 peaches, peeled and sliced

Directions:

1. To prep the apple crumble: In a medium bowl, combine the brown sugar, flour, oats, butter, cinnamon, nutmeg, and salt and mix well. The mixture will be dry and crumbly.
2. To prep the peach crumble: In a medium bowl, combine the brown sugar, flour, oats, butter, cinnamon, and salt and mix well. The mixture will be dry and crumbly.
3. To cook both crumbles: Spread the apples in the Zone 1 basket in an even layer. Top evenly with the apple crumble topping and insert the basket in the unit. Spread the peaches in the Zone 2 basket in an even layer. Top with the peach crumble topping and insert the basket in the unit.
4. Select Zone 1, select BAKE, set the temperature to 350°F, and set the timer to 20 minutes. Select MATCH COOK to match Zone 2 settings to Zone 1.
5. Press START/PAUSE to begin cooking.
6. When cooking is complete, the fruit will be tender and the crumble topping crisp and golden brown. Serve warm or at room temperature.

Nutrition:

- (Per serving) Calories: 300; Total fat: 6.5g; Saturated fat: 3.5g; Carbohydrates: 59g; Fiber: 5.5g; Protein: 2g; Sodium: 45mg

Fluffy Layered Peanut Butter Cheesecake Brownies

Servings: 6

Cooking Time: 35 Minutes

Ingredients:

- ½ cup blanched finely ground almond flour
- 1 cup powdered erythritol, divided
- 2 tablespoons unsweetened cocoa powder
- ½ teaspoon baking powder
- ¼ cup unsalted butter, softened
- 2 large eggs, divided
- 8 ounces full-fat cream cheese, softened
- ¼ cup heavy whipping cream
- 1 teaspoon vanilla extract
- 2 tablespoons no-sugar-added peanut butter

Directions:

1. In a large bowl, combine ½ cup erythritol, almond flour, baking powder and cocoa powder. Add in butter and one egg, stir well.
2. Spoon mixture into 6&quot| round baking pan. Put pan into the air fryer basket.
3. Set the temperature to 300°F, then set the timer for 20 minutes.
4. A toothpick inserted in center will come out clean when fully cooked. Allow to completely cool for 20 minutes and firm up.
5. In a large bowl, beat heavy cream, cream cheese, remaining ½ cup erythritol, peanut butter, remaining egg, and vanilla until turns fluffy.
6. Spoon mixture over cooled brownies. Return the pan into the air fryer basket.
7. Set the temperature to 300°F, then set the timer for 15 minutes.
8. When fully done, cheesecake will be slightly browned and mostly firm with
9. a slight jiggle. Let it rest and refrigerate for at least 2 hours before serving.

Honeyed, Roasted Apples With Walnuts & Rhubarb And Strawberry Crumble

Servings: 10

Cooking Time: 12 To 17 Minutes

Ingredients:

- Honeyed, Roasted Apples with Walnuts:
- 2 Granny Smith apples
- 20 g certified gluten-free rolled oats
- 2 tablespoons honey
- ½ teaspoon ground cinnamon
- 2 tablespoons chopped walnuts
- Pinch salt
- 1 tablespoon olive oil
- Rhubarb and Strawberry Crumble:
- 250 g sliced fresh strawberries
- 95 g sliced rhubarb
- 75 g granulated sugar
- 60 g quick-cooking oatmeal
- 50 g whole-wheat pastry flour, or plain flour
- 50 g packed light brown sugar
- ½ teaspoon ground cinnamon
- 3 tablespoons unsalted butter, melted

Directions:

1. Make the Honeyed, Roasted Apples with Walnuts :
2. Preheat the air fryer to 190°C.
3. Core the apples and slice them in half.
4. In a medium bowl, mix together the oats, honey, cinnamon, walnuts, salt, and olive oil.
5. Scoop a quarter of the oat mixture onto the top of each half apple.
6. Place the apples in the zone 1 air fryer basket, and roast for 12 to 15 minutes, or until the apples are fork tender.
7. Make the Rhubarb and Strawberry Crumble :
8. Preheat the air fryer to 190°C.
9. In a 6-by-2-inch round metal baking pan, combine the strawberries, rhubarb, and granulated sugar.
10. In a medium bowl, stir together the oatmeal, flour, brown sugar, and cinnamon. Stir the melted butter into this mixture until crumbly. Sprinkle the crumble mixture over the fruit.
11. Once the unit is preheated, place the pan into the zone 2 basket.
12. Bake for 12 minutes then check the crumble. If the fruit is bubbling and the topping is golden brown, it is done. If not, resume cooking.
13. When the cooking is complete, serve warm.

Berry Crumble And S'mores

Servings: 8
Cooking Time: 15 Minutes

Ingredients:

- Berry Crumble:
- For the Filling:
- 300 g mixed berries
- 2 tablespoons sugar
- 1 tablespoon cornflour
- 1 tablespoon fresh lemon juice
- For the Topping:
- 30 g plain flour
- 20 g rolled oats
- 1 tablespoon granulated sugar
- 2 tablespoons cold unsalted butter, cut into small cubes
- Whipped cream or ice cream (optional)
- S'mores:
- Coconut, or avocado oil, for spraying
- 8 digestive biscuits
- 2 (45 g) chocolate bars
- 4 large marshmallows

Directions:

1. Make the Berry Crumble :
2. 1. Preheat the air fryer to 204°C. For the filling: In a round baking pan, gently mix the berries, sugar, cornflour, and lemon juice until thoroughly combined. 3. For the topping: In a small bowl, combine the flour, oats, and sugar. Stir the butter into the flour mixture until the mixture has the consistency of breadcrumbs. 4. Sprinkle the topping over the berries. 5. Put the pan in the zone 1 air fryer drawer and air fry for 15 minutes. Let cool for 5 minutes on a wire rack. 6. Serve topped with whipped cream or ice cream, if desired.
3. Make the S'mores :
4. Line the zone 2 air fryer drawer with baking paper and spray lightly with oil.
5. Place 4 biscuits into the prepared drawer.
6. Break the chocolate bars in half, and place 1/2 on top of each biscuit. Top with 1 marshmallow.
7. Air fry at 188°C for 30 seconds, or until the marshmallows are puffed, golden brown and slightly melted.
8. Top with the remaining biscuits and serve.

Apple Nutmeg Flautas

Servings: 8
Cooking Time: 8 Minutes.

Ingredients:

- ¼ cup light brown sugar
- ⅛ cup all-purpose flour
- ¼ teaspoon ground cinnamon
- Nutmeg, to taste
- 4 apples, peeled, cored & sliced
- ½ lemon, juice, and zest
- 6 (10-inch) flour tortillas
- Vegetable oil
- Caramel sauce
- Cinnamon sugar

Directions:

1. Mix brown sugar with cinnamon, nutmeg, and flour in a large bowl.
2. Toss in apples in lemon juice. Mix well.
3. Place a tortilla at a time on a flat surface and add ½ cup of the apple mixture to the tortilla.
4. Roll the tortilla into a burrito and seal it tightly and hold it in place with a toothpick.
5. Repeat the same steps with the remaining tortillas and apple mixture.
6. Place two apple burritos in each of the crisper plate and spray them with cooking oil.
7. Return the crisper plates to the Ninja Foodi Dual Zone Air Fryer.
8. Choose the Air Fry mode for Zone 1 and set the temperature to 400 degrees F and the time to 8 minutes.
9. Select the "MATCH" button to copy the settings for Zone 2.
10. Initiate cooking by pressing the START/STOP button.
11. Flip the burritos once cooked halfway through, then resume cooking.
12. Garnish with caramel sauce and cinnamon sugar.
13. Enjoy!

Nutrition:

- (Per serving) Calories 157 | Fat 1.3g |Sodium 27mg | Carbs 1.3g | Fiber 1g | Sugar 2.2g | Protein 8.2g

Crustless Peanut Butter Cheesecake And Pumpkin Pudding With Vanilla Wafers

Servings: 6
Cooking Time: 17 Minutes

Ingredients:

- Crustless Peanut Butter Cheesecake:
- 110 g cream cheese, softened
- 2 tablespoons powdered sweetener
- 1 tablespoon all-natural, no-sugar-added peanut butter
- ½ teaspoon vanilla extract
- 1 large egg, whisked
- Pumpkin Pudding with Vanilla Wafers:
- 250 g canned no-salt-added pumpkin purée (not pumpkin pie filling)
- 50 g packed brown sugar
- 3 tablespoons plain flour
- 1 egg, whisked
- 2 tablespoons milk
- 1 tablespoon unsalted butter, melted
- 1 teaspoon pure vanilla extract
- 4 low-fat vanilla, or plain wafers, crumbled
- Nonstick cooking spray

Directions:

1. Make the Crustless Peanut Butter Cheesecake :
2. In a medium bowl, mix cream cheese and sweetener until smooth. Add peanut butter and vanilla, mixing until smooth. Add egg and stir just until combined.
3. Spoon mixture into an ungreased springform pan and place into the zone 1 air fryer drawer. Adjust the temperature to 148°C and bake for 10 minutes. Edges will be firm, but center will be mostly set with only a small amount of jiggle when done.
4. Let pan cool at room temperature 30 minutes, cover with plastic wrap, then place into refrigerator at least 2 hours. Serve chilled.
5. Make the Pumpkin Pudding with Vanilla Wafers :
6. Preheat the air fryer to 176°C. Coat a baking pan with nonstick cooking spray. Set aside.
7. Mix the pumpkin purée, brown sugar, flour, whisked egg, milk, melted butter, and vanilla in a medium bowl and whisk to combine. Transfer the mixture to the baking pan.
8. Place the baking pan in the zone 2 air fryer drawer and bake for 12 to 17 minutes until set.
9. Remove the pudding from the drawer to a wire rack to cool.
10. Divide the pudding into four bowls and serve with the vanilla wafers sprinkled on top.

Apple Crisp

Servings: 8
Cooking Time: 15 Minutes

Ingredients:

- 3 cups apples, chopped
- 1 tablespoon pure maple syrup
- 2 teaspoons lemon juice
- 3 tablespoons all-purpose flour
- ⅓ cup quick oats
- ¼ cup brown sugar
- 2 tablespoons light butter, melted
- ½ teaspoon cinnamon

Directions:

1. Toss the chopped apples with 1 tablespoon of all-purpose flour, cinnamon, maple syrup, and lemon juice in a suitable bowl.
2. Divide the apples in the two air fryer baskets with their crisper plates.
3. Whisk oats, brown sugar, and remaining all-purpose flour in a small bowl.
4. Stir in melted butter, then divide this mixture over the apples.
5. Return the crisper plate to the Ninja Foodi Dual Zone Air Fryer.
6. Select the Bake mode for Zone 1 and set the temperature to 375 degrees F and the time to 14 minutes.
7. Select the “MATCH” button to copy the settings for Zone 2.
8. Initiate cooking by pressing the START/STOP button.
9. Enjoy fresh.

Air Fried Beignets

Servings: 6

Cooking Time: 17 Minutes.

Ingredients:

- Cooking spray
- ¼ cup white sugar
- ⅛ cup water
- ½ cup all-purpose flour
- 1 large egg, separated
- 1 ½ teaspoons butter, melted
- ½ teaspoon baking powder
- ½ teaspoon vanilla extract
- 1 pinch salt
- 2 tablespoons confectioners' sugar, or to taste

Directions:

1. Beat flour with water, sugar, egg yolk, baking powder, butter, vanilla extract, and salt in a large bowl until lumps-free.
2. Beat egg whites in a separate bowl and beat using an electric hand mixer until it forms soft peaks.
3. Add the egg white to the flour batter and mix gently until fully incorporated.
4. Divide the dough into small beignets and place them in the crisper plate.
5. Return the crisper plate to the Ninja Foodi Dual Zone Air Fryer.
6. Choose the Air Fry mode for Zone 1 and set the temperature to 390 degrees F and the time to 17 minutes.
7. Select the "MATCH" button to copy the settings for Zone 2.
8. Initiate cooking by pressing the START/STOP button.
9. And cook for another 4 minutes. Dust the cooked beignets with sugar.
10. Serve.

Nutrition:

- (Per serving) Calories 327 | Fat 14.2g |Sodium 672mg | Carbs 47.2g | Fiber 1.7g | Sugar 24.8g | Protein 4.4g

Mini Blueberry Pies

Servings: 2

Cooking Time: 15 Minutes

Ingredients:

- 1 box store-bought pie dough, Trader Joe's
- ¼ cup blueberry jam
- 1 teaspoon lemon zest
- 1 egg white, for brushing

Directions:

1. Take the store-bought pie dough and cut it into 3-inch circles.
2. Brush the dough with egg white all around the edges.
3. Now add blueberry jam and zest in the middle and top it with another circle.
4. Press the edges with a fork to seal it.
5. Make a slit in the middle of each pie and divide them between the baskets.
6. Set zone 1 to AIR FRY mode 360 degrees for 10 minutes.
7. Select the MATCH button for zone 2.
8. Once cooked, serve.

Pumpkin Cookie With Cream Cheese Frosting

Servings: 6

Cooking Time: 7 Minutes

Ingredients:

- 50 g blanched finely ground almond flour
- 50 g powdered sweetener, divided
- 2 tablespoons butter, softened
- 1 large egg
- ½ teaspoon unflavored gelatin
- ½ teaspoon baking powder
- ½ teaspoon vanilla extract
- ½ teaspoon pumpkin pie spice
- 2 tablespoons pure pumpkin purée
- ½ teaspoon ground cinnamon, divided
- 40 g low-carb, sugar-free chocolate chips
- 85 g full-fat cream cheese, softened

Directions:

1. In a large bowl, mix almond flour and 25 gsweetener. Stir in butter, egg, and gelatin until combined. 2. Stir in baking powder, vanilla, pumpkin pie spice, pumpkin purée, and ¼ teaspoon cinnamon, then fold in chocolate chips. 3. Pour batter into a round baking pan. Place pan into the zone 1 air fryer basket. 4. Adjust the temperature to 150°C and bake for 7 minutes. 5. When fully cooked, the top will be golden brown, and a toothpick inserted in center will come out clean. Let cool at least 20 minutes. 6. To make the frosting: mix cream cheese, remaining ¼ teaspoon cinnamon, and remaining 25 g sweetener in a large bowl. Using an electric mixer, beat until it becomes fluffy. Spread onto the cooled cookie. Garnish with additional cinnamon if desired.

Monkey Bread

Servings: 12

Cooking Time: 10 Minutes

Ingredients:

- Bread
- 12 Rhodes white dinner rolls
- ½ cup brown sugar
- 1 teaspoon cinnamon
- 4 tablespoons butter melted
- Glaze
- ½ cup powdered sugar
- 1-2 tablespoons milk
- ½ teaspoon vanilla

Directions:

1. Mix brown sugar, cinnamon and butter in a bowl.
2. Cut the dinner rolls in half and dip them in the sugar mixture.
3. Place these buns in a greased baking pan and pour the remaining butter on top.
4. Place the buns in the air fryer baskets.
5. Return the air fryer basket 1 to Zone 1, and basket 2 to Zone 2 of the Ninja Foodi 2-Basket Air Fryer.
6. Choose the "Air Fry" mode for Zone 1 at 350 degrees F and 10 minutes of cooking time.
7. Initiate cooking by pressing the START/PAUSE BUTTON.
8. Flip the rolls once cooked halfway through.
9. Meanwhile, mix milk, vanilla and sugar in a bowl.
10. Pour the glaze over the air fried rolls.
11. Serve.

Nutrition:

- (Per serving) Calories 192 | Fat 9.3g |Sodium 133mg | Carbs 27.1g | Fiber 1.4g | Sugar 19g | Protein 3.2g

RECIPES INDEX

A

Air Fried Bacon And Eggs 24

Air Fried Bananas 91

Air Fried Beignets 100

Air Fried Chicken Potatoes With Sun-dried Tomato 76

Air Fried Okra 40

Air Fryer Sausage Patties 28

Air Fryer Vegetables 36

Air-fried Tofu Cutlets With Cacio E Pepe Brussels Sprouts 38

Apple Crisp 99

Apple Crumble Peach Crumble 96

Apple Nutmeg Flautas 98

Asian Pork Skewers 46

Asparagus And Bell Pepper Strata And Greek Bagels 26

Avocado Fries 31

B

Bacon And Egg Omelet 28

Bacon Cheese Egg With Avocado And Potato Nuggets 17

Bacon Cinnamon Rolls 17

Bacon-wrapped Chicken 81

Bacon-wrapped Shrimp And Jalapeño 33

Baked Egg And Mushroom Cups 19

Baked Eggs 23

Bang-bang Chicken 75

Basil Cheese Salmon 59

Bbq Corn 36

Bbq Pork Loin 48

Beef & Broccoli 52

Beef Ribs Ii 49

Beefy Swiss Pastry 32

Beer Battered Fish Fillet 65

Berry Crumble And S'mores 98

Blackened Red Snapper 63

Breaded Pork Chops 45

Breakfast Meatballs 23

Breakfast Sausage And Cauliflower 27

Breakfast Sausage Omelet 16

Broccoli And Cheese Stuffed Chicken 85

Broccoli Cheese Chicken 78

Broiled Teriyaki Salmon With Eggplant In Stir-fry Sauce 63

Brussels Sprouts Potato Hash 25

Buffalo Bites 40

Buffalo Chicken Breakfast Muffins 15

Butter Cake 93

Butter-wine Baked Salmon 67

C

Cajun Scallops 61

Caramelized Onion Dip With White Cheese 31

Cheese Corn Fritters 35

Cheesy Low-carb Lasagna 50

Chicken And Broccoli 83

Chicken And Vegetable Fajitas 74

Chicken Breast Strips 79

Chicken Fajitas With Street Corn 72

Chicken Legs With Leeks 88

Chicken Parmesan With Roasted Lemon-parmesan Broccoli 84

Chicken Potatoes 73

Chicken Strips With Satay Sauce 78

Chicken Stuffed Mushrooms 29

Chicken Tenders And Curly Fries 87

Chicken Wings With Piri Piri Sauce 77

Chicken With Pineapple And Peach 75

Chili Chicken Wings 83

Chili Honey Salmon 65

Chili Lime Tilapia 67

Chipotle Beef 56

Chocolate Cookies 93

Chocolate Pudding 92

Cinnamon Air Fryer Apples 27

Cinnamon Apple French Toast 22

Cinnamon Bread Twists 95

Cinnamon Sugar Dessert Fries 90

Cinnamon-apple Pork Chops 53

Cinnamon-beef Kofta 52

Citrus Mousse 91

Coconut Muffins And Dark Chocolate Lava Cake 91

Cod With Avocado And Garlic Prawns 70

Cod With Jalapeño 57

Crab Rangoon Dip With Crispy Wonton Strips 30

Crispy Filo Artichoke Triangles 35

Crispy Fish Nuggets 68

Crispy Hash Browns 21

Crispy Parmesan Cod 71

Crumb-topped Sole 64

Crusted Chicken Breast 84

Crusted Cod 65

Crusted Shrimp 67

Crustless Peanut Butter Cheesecake And Pumpkin Pudding With Vanilla Wafers 99

Curly Fries 37

Curried Orange Honey Chicken 75

Curry-crusted Lamb Chops With Baked Brown Sugar Acorn Squash 50

D

Delicious Chicken Skewers 79

Dijon Chicken Wings 82

Double Chocolate Brownies 88

Dukkah-crusted Halibut 64

E

Easy Breaded Pork Chops 56

Easy Mini Chocolate Chip Pan Cookie 94

Egg And Bacon Muffins 21

Eggs In Avocado Cups 25

F

Falafel 39

Fish And Chips 64

Five-ingredient Falafel With Garlic-yoghurt Sauce 32

Flavorful Salmon With Green Beans 60

Fluffy Layered Peanut Butter Cheesecake Brownies 97

Fried Asparagus 37

Fried Okra 34

Fried Olives 40
Fried Prawns 58
Frozen Breaded Fish Fillet 71

G

Garlic Butter Steak Bites 45
Garlic Dill Wings 86
Garlic Sirloin Steak 47
General Tso's Chicken 76
Goat Cheese-stuffed Bavette Steak 52
Greek Chicken Souvlaki 79
Green Pepper Cheeseburgers 54
Gyro Breakfast Patties With Tzatziki 18

H

Hard Boiled Eggs 18
Hash Browns 15
Hasselback Potatoes 39
Healthy Oatmeal Muffins 21
Healthy Spinach Balls 36
Herb And Lemon Cauliflower 38
Herbed Prawns Pita 61
Herbed Turkey Breast With Simple Dijon Sauce 87
Honey Banana Oatmeal 24
Honey Butter Chicken 73
Honey Glazed Bbq Pork Ribs 49
Honey Teriyaki Salmon 62
Honey-apricot Granola With Greek Yoghurt 25
Honeyed, Roasted Apples With Walnuts & Rhubarb And Strawberry Crumble 97
Hot Dogs Wrapped In Bacon 51

I

Italian Sausages With Peppers And Teriyaki Rump Steak With Broccoli 48
Italian-style Meatballs With Garlicky Roasted Broccoli 55

J

Jerk Chicken Thighs 80
Juicy Paprika Chicken Breast 74

K

Kale And Spinach Chips 39
Kale Potato Nuggets 29

L

Lemon Pepper Fish Fillets 59
Lemon Pepper Salmon With Asparagus 61

M

Marinated Steak & Mushrooms 45
Meat And Rice Stuffed Peppers 53
Meatballs 51
Mini Blueberry Pies 100
Mocha Pudding Cake Vanilla Pudding Cake 95
Moist Chocolate Espresso Muffins 90
Molten Chocolate Almond Cakes 92
Mongolian Beef With Sweet Chili Brussels Sprouts 54
Monkey Bread 101
Morning Egg Rolls 20
Morning Patties 15
Mozzarella Bacon Calzones 22
Mozzarella Sticks 33
Mushroom Rolls 34
Mustard Pork Chops 57
Mustard Rubbed Lamb Chops 57

O

Onion Omelette And Buffalo Egg Cups 20

P

Parmesan Crush Chicken 29

Parmesan French Fries 34

Parmesan Wings 33

Parmesan-crusted Fish Sticks With Baked Macaroni And Cheese 69

Pepper Egg Cups 19

Pepper Poppers 44

Pepperoni Pizza Dip 35

Perfect Parmesan Salmon 66

Pickled Chicken Fillets 81

Pork Tenderloin With Brown Sugar–pecan Sweet Potatoes 55

Pork With Green Beans And Potatoes 47

Potato And Parsnip Latkes With Baked Apples 42

Prawn Dejonghe Skewers 71

Pretzel Chicken Cordon Bleu 85

Pumpkin Cookie With Cream Cheese Frosting 100

Pumpkin Muffins 96

Pumpkin Muffins With Cinnamon 88

Q

Quiche Breakfast Peppers 16

Quick And Easy Blueberry Muffins 18

Quickie Cinnamon Sugar Pork Rinds 94

R

Red Pepper And Feta Frittata And Bacon Eggs On The Go 24

Roasted Beef 51

Rosemary Asparagus & Potatoes 42

S

S'mores Dip With Cinnamon-sugar Tortillas 94

Salmon Nuggets 66

Sausage & Butternut Squash 23

Scallops And Spinach With Cream Sauce And Confetti Salmon Burgers 62

Scallops With Greens 56

Sesame Honey Salmon 69

Shrimp Pirogues 30

Simple Beef Sirloin Roast 49

Simple Buttery Cod & Salmon On Bed Of Fennel And Carrot 66

Simple Lamb Meatballs 51

Simply Terrific Turkey Meatballs 73

Snapper Scampi 63

South Indian Fried Fish 60

Southwestern Fish Fillets 69

Spanakopita Rolls With Mediterranean Vegetable Salad 41

Spiced Apple Cake 93

Spiced Chicken And Vegetables 86

Spice-rubbed Chicken Pieces 72

Spicy Chicken Sandwiches With "fried" Pickles 77

Spicy Salmon Fillets 60

Spinach And Red Pepper Egg Cups With Coffee-glazed Canadian Bacon 27

Spinach And Swiss Frittata With Mushrooms 28

Spinach Egg Muffins 19

Steak And Mashed Creamy Potatoes 46

Steak In Air Fry 46

Stuffed Apples 92

Stuffed Chicken Florentine 85

Stuffed Mushrooms With Crab 68

Stuffed Sweet Potatoes 37

Stuffed Tomatoes 41

Sweet Potato Hash 23

Sweet Potatoes With Honey Butter 44

Sweet Protein Powder Doughnut Holes 90

T

Taco Seasoned Steak 53

Tater Tots 31

Tender Pork Chops 47

Thai Chicken Meatballs 82

Thai Curry Chicken Kabobs 80

Tilapia With Mojo And Crispy Plantains 58

Tuna Patties With Spicy Sriracha Sauce Coconut Prawns 59

Turkey And Cranberry Quesadillas 82

Turkey Burger Patties 80

Turkey Ham Muffins 22

Two-way Salmon 68

V

Veggie Burgers With “fried” Onion Rings 43

Victoria Sponge Cake 89

W

Whole Chicken 74

Wholemeal Banana-walnut Bread 16

Wings With Corn On Cob 87

Y

Yellow Potatoes With Eggs 26

Yummy Chicken Breasts 86

Z

Zesty Cranberry Scones 89

Zucchini Cakes 43

Printed in Great Britain
by Amazon

37952004R00059